AF680132

Blue Line Rogue

Corruption in Georgia

Double Duck Productions
An imprint of IFG Holdings, LLC
1628 E. Southern Ave, #9-322
Tempe, AZ 85282
www.doubleduckproductions.com

Blue Line Rogue: Corruption in Georgia
[3rd Edition]

Simultaneously published globally by Double Duck Productions

Copyright © 2024 Double Duck Productions; all rights reserved
Copyright © 2024 John Masters; all rights reserved
www.bluelinerogue.com

Double Duck Productions supports copyright laws and the intellectual property of it's creators. Copyright protection drives imagination, encourages diversity and inclusion, protects free speech, and allows all cultures to have a voice and be heard. Thank you for purchasing an authorized edition of this book, and for observing copyright and intellectual property laws by not reproducing, scanning, or distributing any part of it in any manner or form without permission. You are supporting artists, creators, and writers; and helping Double Duck to continue to publish and produce content for it's contracted creators and authors.

ISBN 979-8-9920412-6-2 (ebook)
ISBN 979-8-9920412-7-9 (paperback)
ISBN 979-8-9920412-8-6 (audiobook)

Printed in the United States of America

Blue Line Rogue

Corruption in Georgia

Author: John Masters

Foreword by: David Larkins

Edited by: Ryan Lassler, Paul Rogers, & Zackery Watson

Cover Design by: Ninu Bebek with John Masters

3rd Edition

www.bluelinerogue.com

This book is dedicated to all those who hold the truth and are not believed...
Always hold onto the truth, no matter what the consequences are.
Thank you, Uncle Dennis, for your influence. I am safer, more competent in my skills because you taught me to rely on myself, and not wait to be picked.

TABLE OF CONTENTS

FOREWORD

Corruption exists. I suppose it is present in most people to some degree. In more than two decades of police work I have seen my share of corruption in a profession which can magnify the worst within a person if that person allows it. I can recall the anger I saw in an officer's face after he looked at me with a wink and said, "I smell marijuana in this car, don't you?"

My negative response was not the one which he was accustomed to hearing. I am reminded of the frustration I felt at seeing a man who I had arrested for DUI working in the hayfield of a local judge. His charges had been dismissed. I recall the helpless feeling of a friend who was arrested by his wife's lover, an officer in the city where they lived. His wife and her lover spent the weekend together while he sat in jail awaiting a bond hearing.

I watched a coworker go to prison after he was caught stealing narcotics from a suspect in order to feed his own hidden addiction. Even though I know corruption exists, it was with skepticism that I first listened to John Masters tell of his experience in Poulan, Georgia.

I first met John Masters when he moved to the area and took a job at Oglethorpe County Sheriff's Office. Having made a career in law enforcement myself, we naturally started talking about our experiences, the calls for service we had answered, the people with whom we had worked, and the departments where we had served. Two things struck me immediately about John.

First was his demeanor. John was upbeat and friendly. His positive outlook on life was contagious and somewhat unusual for a person with a career in law enforcement. He was without the cynical lens through which so many officers view society.

Second, was his commitment to integrity. John is perhaps the most honest person I have encountered in my profession. I did not find any embellishment in his stories. It is almost a point of pride for cops to stretch certain elements of a story to either make themselves appear more heroic, or to enhance the humor already existing in the tale.

When John would relate an experience, it was very matter of fact. Here are the details. This is what happened. The end. He also made no attempt to hide or diminish any detail which may have made him look bad. The truth was more important to John than the perception others had of him. His integrity was of greater value than loyalty to the unwritten code of protecting a fellow cop who doled out extrajudicial punishment to a suspect who "deserved it".

As John related to me the story you will read in this book, I was reading him. I took in every facial expression. I also watched his hands, shoulders, and feet, but it is in a person's face where I can most often detect signs of dishonesty. I can clearly remember at age nine the moment when I knew my best friend had stolen my water gun.

It was missing, and when I asked him about it his face tensed up ever so slightly in a way I had not seen before. Further questioning revealed the truth, and he handed over the toy with an apology. This skill of reading facial expressions and body language became better with training and experience.

It served me well in my career. Now I was putting this skill to use as I listened to John tell me about the corruption he witnessed. Not once did I ever see a single sign of deception. The follow-up questions I posed were answered quickly and clearly. Not a single element of his story ever changed. I am convinced that John was doing his best to tell the truth.

I can say the same about Zack Watson. I interviewed Zack on two occasions. Although different in personality from John, Zack seems to possess the same commitment to the truth as his former coworker. Some minor, inconsequential details were different between the accounts. This is to be expected.

If every single detail was exactly the same, it would raise a red flag and possibly indicate a conspiracy or collaboration between the two. I found no red flags. What I did find was a consistent story, with accord on every significant point.

John and Zack are good, selfless, trustworthy men who had the misfortune of working for someone who was none of those things. Sunlight is nature's disinfectant, and this story is their attempt to expose the corruption they encountered to the sunlight of public view. With enough exposure, perhaps the disinfecting properties of light will help clean up the corruption they uncovered.

- David Larkins

TIMELESS

QUOTES

"Many enter public office with the aim of acquiring goods that they lack... Only those who do not seek power are qualified to hold it…"

- From The Republic, by Plato

"He that is greedy of gain troubles his own house. The heart of the righteous studies to answer: but the mouth of the wicked pours out evil things."

- From Proverbs, by Yedidyah (Solomon)

PREFACE

This book emerged from events that occurred between the spring of 2022 and late fall of 2024, almost three years of collusion among several police executives. The sole purpose of this collusion was to protect a police chief caught tampering with evidence by his own officers. Although several officers were involved or witnessed the events, only one officer chose to pen this book for the public to read and form their own conclusions.

My name is John Masters, and I am a certified police officer in the state of Georgia. Over seven years of service, I have completed over a thousand hours of formalized training in law enforcement. My training includes advanced certifications in speed detection, DUI enforcement, de-escalation, report writing, recognizing mental and developmental disorders, gaining compliance without use of force, narcotics identification, interdiction, roadside interviews, high-risk traffic stops, vehicle pursuits, investigations, and evidence control.

In comparison, my training far surpasses that of Larry Whisenant, the Poulan Police Chief, or Frank Walker, the now-retired Assistant Police Chief. Please understand, this book is not written out of malice but out of a desire to reveal the truth of the events to the public.

For the past two and a half years, my reputation and character have been openly defamed by Larry Whisenant and his associates, Frank Walker and Douglas Dowdy. This campaign of defamation has forced others to either lie for Whisenant or, worse, turn a blind eye to the truth.

Now, after these three men have had ample opportunity to speak their part, it is my turn to share mine. Georgia Peace Officer Standards and Training (POST) chose not to sanction my certification, despite the false and damaging accusations made against me by these three men. This book serves as my opportunity to present my side of the story.

While I was writing this book, I was not actively employed in law enforcement. During that time, I maintained my certification and training at my own expense and on my own personal time. I am now actively employed in law enforcement and continue to expand and maintain my knowledge of case law, statutory law, and modern ethical policing procedures in the United States. Zackery Watson, the other officer who was intimately involved in these events, has been instrumental in writing this book. His perspective has been invaluable, and he has contributed significantly to the editing process to ensure accuracy and provide context regarding the actions of Whisenant, Walker, Dowdy, and others involved.

This book should serve as a warning to rank-and-file officers and, most importantly, to the public at large. I am not suggesting that all law enforcement officers and command staff are untrustworthy. However, in this case, high-ranking officials allowed these individuals unchecked power, enabling them to manipulate documents, control situations, and destroy one officer's career based on demonstrably false statements made by a single police chief.

If they can do this to a police officer with near-total impunity, it is clear that the public will stand little chance against such unchecked power in the future. Everyone should be wary of such power and its potential abuse.

Please read this book with an open heart. What happened here is not the norm in law enforcement. I forgave Larry Whisenant, Frank Walker, and Douglas Dowdy long ago. My faith compels me to hold no grudges; my God demands that I not remain anchored in their mistakes and misery. I understand that I am on a path of eternal progression, and instead of dwelling on them, I release them and their problems with the writing of this book. I choose to follow the law of progression and leave the aftermath in the hands of God, to whom I express my gratitude, satisfaction, and praise.

INTRODUCTION

While this book may seem fantastical, these events actually occurred. This book chronicles several police officers' experiences with the actions of a Southwest Georgia Police Chief and his friend, a Georgia Peace Officer Standards and Training Investigator—actions the Chief took after a single traffic stop.

A series of coincidences led to uncovering deep corruption at both the city and state levels. Consideration must also be given to the additional officer who witnessed much of what occurred but was not in a position to intervene, though he did so anyway. That officer's courage and ethical standards helped the author navigate much of the fallout from the defamation and lies spread by multiple command staff officers and staff at the Georgia Peace Officer Standards and Training (POST).

Although only one of the officers authored this book, it was written from the perspective of all three officers. It is written in the third person to allow the reader to understand the viewpoints, opinions, and emotions of each officer as the facts and circumstances unfolded during this difficult ordeal. The other officers actively participated in the editing process to ensure accuracy and also served as a sounding board for the content and context of the events recounted in this book, as they were active participants.

Please understand that these officers are firm believers that the corruption detailed herein does not represent the normal culture within the vast majority of law enforcement agencies in the United States or even in Georgia. However, they do believe that a culture of "mind your own business" exists to the extent that the public perceives a “blue wall of silence.”

In this case, it seems accurate to say that multiple officers, with the power to act, chose not to—whatever their reasons may have been. The officers do not wish to speculate on the motivations behind these actions but instead rely on the evidence before them. There exists a culture of lying and corruption among certain officers and staff at the Georgia Peace Officer Standards and Training Council.

William of Ockham theorized the principle now known as Occam's Razor—the simplest solution is often the most likely. Walter Chatton, a contemporary of Ockham, disagreed with this notion and coined his own, aptly named "anti-razor." Chatton believed that the world was too complex and full of variables for the truth to be determined by the simplest answer between two questions. He argued that if any version of events did not reveal the truth, more information was needed, and the simplest explanation could not always be the correct one.

It is in the spirit of Chatton that the author has written this book. Please approach it with the understanding that there are at least three sides to every story: two differing versions and the truth.

The author aims to provide a viewpoint of the truth as it occurred and as it was experienced by the two officers involved.

The author also hopes to show the information that led these officers to their conclusions. Regardless of your personal opinions of law enforcement, please remember that the United States is a nation of laws, not armies, and its citizens and law enforcement are supposed to be—and typically are—far more professional and law-abiding than what transpired in the City of Poulan and the State of Georgia during the spring of 2022 and beyond.

This book represents an exception to law enforcement norms, not the rule.

— The Author

PROLOGUE

Spring in South Georgia is a mix of lingering cold and high humidity. Pollen and fog mingle in the early evening, with temperatures that are just uncomfortable enough to make you question whether to wear a jacket. The gnats and mosquitoes come out in full force, seemingly irritated by the impending summer, ready to take out their anger on anyone who dares step outside after a shower.

The Poulan Police Department was small, but not closely-knit, located along the well-known stretch of U.S. Highway 82 between Tifton and Albany. It was the heart of what policing in southwest Georgia looked like—an uneasy blend of small-town politics and the pressure on officers to perform at a high level for financial gain.

The city had earned a reputation throughout the region as a speed trap, with officers rotating in and out every few years. Many used the town only to gain experience before moving on, but a small handful stayed longer than ten years. These long-timers were often eager to join the Police Chief and City Council in their efforts to take advantage of both the local residents and unsuspecting drivers passing through.

For 17 years, the city government had allowed the Police Chief to essentially control the town and its services. The city generated a significant amount of revenue each month, like clockwork, thanks to the police department and its leader.

But things hadn't always been this way. There was a time when the Police Chief was honorable and free of corruption. That changed in late 2007 when the controlling council fired the last Police Chief for doing her job—investigating corruption within the Mayor's Office.

In 2012, the Mayor would be arrested for felony narcotics possession and intent to distribute by a neighboring county. It was suspected that his sources came from the Poulan Police Department, but proving this and infiltrating the network of corruption that Police Chief Larry Whisenant had built was difficult.

Unbeknownst to the officers at the Poulan Police Department, this web of corruption extended to the highest levels of Georgia policing: the Georgia Peace Officer Standards and Training Council (GA POST), the organization responsible for certifying and maintaining police credentials in the state.

On the evening of May 4, 2022, the Poulan officers gathered for their usual monthly meeting. It was held on the first Wednesday, typically after the monthly traffic court session. But this meeting felt different. Tension hung in the air. The Police Chief had stumbled in front of his officers, caught in a serious lie and displaying a lack of basic knowledge of traffic law. His officers began to grow suspicious. Something was wrong.

The Assistant Police Chief remained quiet, as he always did. His silence was often interpreted as wisdom, but in reality, it was ignorance—he had been promoted far beyond his abilities, mainly because he and the Police Chief shared a dubious claim: they both "claimed" to be U.S. Marines.

Neither could provide proof of this, nor did they exhibit the usual signs of actual veterans. This failed to impress the only two remaining officers at the department. Zackery Watson, a seasoned officer with experience in both urban and rural policing, had come to the Poulan Police Department for one reason: quiet, community-centered work. He found neither, and eventually moved out of Poulan to return to his home in Albany and Dougherty County, the very place where his law enforcement career had begun.

Zack remained with the department at the request of a friend, but mentally, he was already preparing to leave. Unbeknownst to the Police Chief, he was planning to walk away over what was already beginning to brew—a scandal that would soon be exposed: his Chief was stealing from the evidence locker, and the Assistant Chief was complicit, covering it up with lies.

John Masters, the only other officer left, was new to policing in Georgia. With military experience, John had actually seen combat overseas—unlike the supposed former Marines in charge of the department. He quickly grew disillusioned with their "tough guy" facade.

John was one of the more proactive officers in the department. However, unlike his superior, who was fixated on meeting a citation quota, John focused on catching actual criminals. Months earlier, he had approached the District Attorney's Office about the quota system and his reluctance to enforce it. They explained that policing in small towns required revenue and that Poulan, being poor, relied on it. He was warned that failure to meet the quota would cost him his career. Sickened by the prospect, John began quietly searching for another department—efforts that were continually thwarted by Larry Whisenant, who refused to lose an officer who helped meet the quota.

The officers were under pressure to write citations. Though he would still focus on actual speeders and those with mechanical violations, he drew a line: he would only stop cars that were genuinely breaking the law.

John also began pulling over Poulan residents, including several city council members: one was caught driving 105 miles per hour in a 35 mph zone—three times the posted limit.

After hitting his citation quota, John would spend the rest of the night performing traffic interdiction on the four-lane highway running through the city. In less than two years at the department, John had made 335 arrests and 140 DUI stops, finding stolen guns, convicted felons with firearms, felony narcotics, and wanted persons with violent warrants.

Like Zack, John had grown suspicious of the Police Chief. That evening began like any other, after the court session, with a local bonding agency treating them to dinner at Dairy Queen—a regular ritual with the officers and court clerk. They discussed the month's events, and the Police Chief made his usual announcements, reiterating the citation quota.

"I need this money. For the city," Larry insisted.

According to the Chief, the city was broke, on the verge of financial ruin. For Larry Whisenant, keeping the roads "safe" meant generating revenue. He had failed at nearly every department he had worked at until he came to Poulan. After over 20 years in law enforcement, Larry had worked at both the Dougherty County Police and the Dougherty County Sheriff's Office, where he had been caught falsifying police reports.

His exaggerated tales of combat in the Marine Corps were equally problematic. Larry claimed to have served in units that never deployed overseas and couldn't even distinguish between the First Gulf War and the Global War on Terror. He could produce no documentation to verify his supposed combat service. His claimed role as a tank commander was also suspect, as such a position was held by commissioned officers, not enlisted personnel. His record in law enforcement was marred by poor case law and a reputation for stealing and lying.

Franklin Walker, the Assistant Chief, also claimed to have served in the Marine Corps, but his story was simply a lie. He claimed he missed

Vietnam because he was ordered onto a different airplane—yet Frank was only about 16 years old when the U.S. began withdrawing from Vietnam in 1973. This didn't stop Frank from spinning elaborate stories of his time stationed in Okinawa and Guam. But when John casually mentioned those places, he quickly realized that Frank had never been to either island. Frank even mistakenly believed that Guam was still under Japanese control, claiming, "We gave it back to them... after the war." John had long given up on Frank by this point.

John had shared his concerns about Larry and Frank's lies with Zack, who was already suspicious. Both of them were at their breaking point with the two corrupt police commanders. They had enjoyed their jobs, but their experiences in law enforcement had been tainted by corruption, and they were exhausted from trying to maintain loyalty to their oaths while dealing with men who had the power to destroy their careers with lies.

That night would prove to be the tipping point. It would decide whether they would maintain their professional discretion or finally confront the Police Chief. This night would mark the beginning of a two-and-a-half-year ordeal involving multiple chiefs and members of GA POST who would lie for Larry and Frank, all at Larry's open and documented request. And all of this, so that Larry Whisenant could tamper with just over 340 grams of a white powdery substance...

CHAPTER 1

The City of Poulan Police Department.

Poulan is a small town located on U.S. Highway 82, situated between Tifton and Albany. Its residents represent the typical makeup of a small Southern town. A significant amount of out-of-area traffic uses this road as a bypass from Interstate 75, heading toward Southwest Georgia and Southern Alabama. A railroad once ran actively through Poulan, and at one point, it served as one of the economic hubs of the region. During the Jim Crow era, Poulan, like many other towns in the Deep South, was segregated. Even in

2020, the remnants of segregated housing were still evident, with two distinct "sides" to the town.

The city's graveyard is home to both Confederate soldiers who were killed in action and Confederate veterans who survived the war and returned to the region. Poulan was meant to be like other post-Civil War towns—places where those who fought against the federal government could rebuild their lives, free from the changes being enforced by the victorious Union. These towns, like Poulan, were seen as sanctuaries from what was perceived as "carpet-bagging Yankees," where local governments could control their own fate, away from the "meddling" of the federal government.

In the early 20th century, lynchings occurred in the area, and Poulan, along with neighboring Sylvester, witnessed the arrest of Dr. Martin Luther King Jr. in Albany, Georgia, just one county away. The Civil Rights Movement had a presence in the region during the 1960s and 1970s.

Larry Whisenant, the Police Chief, was quite proud of the town's Confederate legacy. He openly told officers in public meetings and private internal strategy sessions that "the war was not over" (referring to the U.S. Civil War). As an openly admitted neo-Confederate, Poulan was one of the few places where he could hold a position as a police officer, let alone a Police Chief. His views were explicitly racist—he instructed his officers not to pull over "pretty little white girls" and instead "focus on thugs," a racial euphemism used for Black men.

At least once, Larry helped a white woman avoid charges after she was found in possession of a stolen firearm. Despite her arrest, she never faced consequences, and the gun mysteriously disappeared into the evidence locker. On another occasion, he handed a firearm to a convicted domestic violence offender, a federal crime. When this was brought to his attention, all traces of the incident were erased, including the report documenting the transfer of the weapon.

Larry would berate his officers for pulling over his "friends" (who were always white or fellow officers). He told his officers they needed to develop empathy—specifically, empathy for white drivers involved in complaints. His documentation was sparse, and when he did make a traffic stop, he would often call one of his officers to come to his location to write the ticket, illegally detaining the driver until the officer arrived. He feigned a commitment to community policing by organizing events around holidays but ensured that Black residents were either ignored or excluded from taking active roles in city festivals.

Larry Whisenant lived in a new world, and though cautious in his application of racism, he was careful in his conduct. He was a "law and order" chief, but this was not applied equally to everyone in the city. The police department faced a persistent problem: long-term retention of officers was virtually non-existent. Every 4-5 years, the department would hire new personnel. This cycle, though bothersome to residents, was important to Larry. As officers learned more about the town's political environment, they would quietly leave, abandoning Poulan and its government to its own devices.

Larry's name was rarely attached to anything official. He avoided court, except for the monthly city court that he controlled along with the city solicitor. He directed his officers to handle cases within the city limits, keeping felonies and family violence charges off the record, altering citations or using city ordinance "catch-alls" to sidestep state law requirements. "Keep it in the city," Larry would say. In court, he and the city solicitor would alter speeding citations, changing the original charge to something that wouldn't affect the state's budget for speeding-related fines, while the driver still paid the full amount.

Larry enjoyed a level of fear and control over Poulan and its surroundings. He openly controlled public works, the police department, and the fire department, and wielded influence over other departments by controlling hiring and firing processes. He was the enforcer for the City Council, and his open corruption became common knowledge among residents who could do nothing about it.

The lack of long-term retention in the police department was directly tied to Larry Whisenant. His name itself was a fabrication—he had borrowed the name "Larry" from his father, Stephen L. Whisenant, to avoid the reputation he had built as a thief and liar in his younger years. When he joined the Dougherty County Police Department, his reputation as a troublemaker followed him. He struggled with report writing to the point that he employed his spouse to handle the reports for him. Eventually, he was reassigned to another agency. He should have been fired from the Dougherty County Police Department.

Multiple news agencies attempted to expose the open corruption in Poulan, but their efforts were stymied. The city attorney, Tommy Coleman, a former mayor of Albany, was well-versed in using small towns' resources to generate revenue. Though larger cities had dismissed Coleman for his aggressive and often illegal tactics, smaller towns like Poulan relied on his methods to protect them from prosecution.

Coleman's son, Flynn, served as the Poulan City Solicitor, enjoying his position in the scheme. He spent most of his time in the monthly traffic court, working with Larry to alter citations so they wouldn't affect the city's budget. The city wanted their money, and officers unknowingly participated in the racket. Coleman, like Larry Whisenant, had connections within the Georgia Peace Officer Standards and Training (POST) to ensure that officers complied with the scheme.

On night shifts, Larry instructed his officers to take cash bonds in place of court appearances, placing the money in an envelope under his door. Larry was trusted to process these payments, but as time went on, officers began to notice that the tickets and money were never processed. Larry was also known to take bribes, reducing or eliminating tickets for cash. Drivers would pay him directly, and officers overheard these conversations, with some even hearing it from other law enforcement agencies.

The bribes were pocketed, never reported, and the whole process was an open secret. Tickets, arrests, and charges mirrored the demographics of the town—around 60% white. Yet, almost 90% of court appearances involved Black residents, and non-residents. Locals had their charges "handled." Officers and city employees who didn't comply with this system were ousted without warning. The POST investigators assigned to these cases would fabricate reports, destroying the careers of any officer who dared to speak out.

This was Poulan, Georgia, in the spring of 2020.

CHAPTER 2

The Traffic Stop

The weather on April 8, 2022, was ideal for spring in southwest Georgia, a perfect 72 degrees Fahrenheit. The wind blew gently from the west-southwest, making the day feel comfortable despite the usual humidity of the region. As the weekend began in Poulan, GA, the local police force was out in full force with two officers on the road, overlapping shifts, as opposed to the usual single officer.

Zackery Watson had just completed a traffic stop when his partner, John Masters, noticed a suspicious vehicle heading eastbound on U.S. Highway 82, approaching Poulan. The driver appeared distracted, eating with both hands while attempting to drive. When John made eye contact with her, she quickly put the food down, but by then, the vehicle had already crossed over the rumble strips, producing the telltale sound.

John stayed outside his patrol vehicle, continuing to observe. The driver kept glancing at the two patrol cars behind her through her side-view mirrors, her attention completely off the road. More rumble strip noises followed, and then John watched as the vehicle's passenger tires hit the grass. Deciding to initiate a stop, he merged back into traffic. Once he turned around, he quickly caught up to the silver Ford Taurus with Florida plates and entered the tag number into his mobile data computer.

The tag matched a Florida driver, and the system indicated that her license was suspended. John was now certain of the traffic stop's validity. He activated his emergency lights and initiated the stop. For John, no traffic stop was routine. He approached each one uniquely—usually upbeat and non-confrontational—and always introduced himself by his first name to help ease the situation.

He believed in keeping things calm and avoiding escalation.

John had a particular method of approaching vehicle stops. Partly due to his training and experience, he always approached from the passenger side of the vehicle. This allowed him to see everything inside the car, gave him a retreat path in case anything went wrong, and provided greater safety from passing traffic.

The name on the suspended license matched that of the driver. As he approached the car, John immediately smelled marijuana, which was illegal in Georgia. There was also drug paraphernalia in plain sight on the front seat. Although he had probable cause to search the vehicle, John remained calm and simply asked the driver to step out of the car. What the driver didn't know was that she was already going to be arrested for the suspended license.

John preferred not to escalate things at the roadside. He had learned to incorporate drivers and occupants into relaxed conversations during roadside interviews. While he didn't promise warnings, he would often tell drivers, "... as long as your license is valid and nothing else is going on, it'll be a warning—no court, no fine." This simple statement put 99% of drivers at ease, helping John keep things professional and calm.

John's de-escalation training, which emphasized a calm voice and rapport-building, proved effective in many situations. He did his job with a smile when possible. He explained to the driver that her license was suspended in Florida, speaking in a calm tone that was partly sympathetic, though unnecessary. The driver already knew about the suspension and had hoped she might get off the hook. She had been driving on the suspended license for some time, but John was bound by Georgia law and could not simply let her go.

According to Georgia statute, he could not accept a suspended license as bail. John arrested her without hesitation. Zack Watson arrived on the scene shortly after hearing John's radio call about the arrest. John proceeded to read the driver her Miranda rights.

John was strict about Miranda rights, taking the case law literally. His constitutional views had been shaped during his time serving in Iraq and Afghanistan, where he adopted a constructionist interpretation of the Constitution, favoring limited government. While John had previously identified as a Democrat, his social views remained liberal. However, he was still firmly grounded in his interpretation of the Constitution.

To John, the reading of Miranda was not just a formality, but a critical part of respecting individual rights when someone is in custody. He believed privacy rights were unquestionable and should be upheld, especially when someone was no longer free to leave. His strict observance of these rights often made his fellow officers uneasy, but John believed no officer should talk to someone who is in custody without first warning them of their rights.

This made him stand out from other officers, especially when handling situations like this. After reading the driver her Miranda warning, John did something that most officers didn't: he engaged her in conversation. They discussed her trip, her destination, her job, and the items in her car—no yelling, no judgment, just a calm, professional dialogue.

Most people didn't know, but John was only half-American. He had been born in the United States to an American mother. His father, a dual citizen from Canada, had joined the U.S. Air Force in 1972. His grandfather had served in the U.S. Army Air Corps during WWII and was born in Saskatchewan, Canada. This upbringing in the Midwest shaped John's views on many issues, including marijuana and alcohol.

In Alaska, where marijuana and alcohol were legal and barely regulated, John was considered a "square" for not using either substance. However, by the standards of the contiguous U.S., John was seen as liberal—someone who believed in leaving others alone as long as they weren't harming anyone. Yet, in Georgia, where the law was stricter, John enforced the rules because he believed in the supremacy of the law, even if it conflicted with his personal views.

He didn't let his personal preferences influence his actions as a law enforcement officer. He believed in the rule of law and did his duty, even if his heart wasn't always in agreement with it.

Both John and Zack shared a similar belief in upholding the law. They were committed to enforcing the statutes, regardless of their personal feelings, because they believed that the legislature created the law for a reason, and it was their duty to enforce it impartially, without bias or favoritism.

As John continued to talk with the driver, Zack completed his search of the vehicle. The driver was surprisingly honest, even admitting she was transporting pills across state lines from Alabama to Florida. John returned to assist Zack with a systematic search of the car. Zack suddenly called out, having found something. John had already discovered a bag of hydrocodones and drug paraphernalia in the front passenger area. Zack had been searching the trunk when he found a large bag of white powder hidden beneath hair products.

The car was towed to the city impound, and John transported the driver to jail. Back at the station, they processed the evidence: 26 hydrocodone pills, 5.6 grams of marijuana, and over 12 ounces of the white powder.

Using two Scott reagent tests, one of which had been modified, they tested the white powder.

The first test was positive for cocaine, and the second test confirmed it. Warrants were applied for and granted after the judge reviewed the evidence.

When they informed their supervisor, Larry Whisenant, of the developments, he gave the unusual instruction to leave the evidence bags unsealed. This was a red flag for Zack and John, but they couldn't have known at the time that this would be the first sign of Larry's involvement in tampering with evidence.

CHAPTER 3

Tampering With Evidence

The next day, Zack and John found themselves overlapping shifts once again. It was a simple strategy that allowed more police presence on the road without sacrificing officers' off days. This required careful coordination and communication between the shifts. When it came to traffic interdiction, the units were typically smaller than a full patrol shift, demanding even more precise timing and coordination to maximize success within the short overlap.

In Poulan, however, a typical shift consisted of just one officer working a 12-hour period. The concept of overlapping shifts was sold to officers as a "safety-corridor" initiative—a method to enhance road safety for the residents of Poulan, who were supposedly at risk from non-residents recklessly driving through town with drugs and guns. But, as the officers would soon discover, the true motive was a massive increase in citations and seizures, all masked under the guise of road safety.

The weather that day was just as beautiful as the day before. Zack and John had been proactive, and with the surge in weekend traffic, they were making great stops. This included the one they were handling now. They had just arrested a Georgia Department of Corrections (DOC) employee caught with marijuana and an edged weapon—one that the employee admitted to taking from an inmate. Instead of turning it over to the facility, the employee had kept it and now had it in the vehicle that Zack had stopped.

In the middle of this stop, Larry Whisenant pulled up in his personal vehicle, dressed in civilian clothes. It was almost 6:00 pm. Larry seemed nervous. He wanted to ensure the evidence hadn't been sealed—an outright violation of proper police procedure. He also insisted on "re-testing" the substance. John and Zack were already concerned. Larry fumbled his words. The body cameras were rolling, and Larry knew this was the beginning of a serious lie he would need to sell, not just to Zack and John, but to state authorities as well. Everything depended on this moment.

Ultimately, Larry had nothing to worry about. Most state authorities would either ignore Larry's calls or not return them. His lie preparation would be unnecessary, but it would become critical for John and Zack later. It would help prove that Larry was using his connections with Georgia POST and other high-ranking individuals to destroy their careers—or at least try to.

Larry awkwardly stammered that he wanted to make sure no "egg" would be thrown on John and Zack's faces. He told them that the District Attorney, Bryce Johnson, had "concerns" about John. Larry looked uneasy as he continued spinning his lie. This was news to both John and Zack. John had been in near-constant contact with Assistant District Attorney Sandra Guest about his cases, and she had never expressed any concerns. Quite the opposite—she had been encouraging about the accuracy and efficiency of his work.

Larry had a device in mind for delivering these remarks, but in his own mindset, he (like most Southern cops) would never have approached the ADA to ask what went wrong and how to fix it. This was a bully tactic, and it would backfire on Larry. John, raised in the Midwest and having lived in Alaska, wanted to repair the relationship immediately, as Larry claimed it had somehow soured.

In Alaska, relationships meant everything. When temperatures dropped below -30°F, bad relationships meant being shut out from both hearth and home. John was direct, simple to a fault—a trait that placed him at a great disadvantage in the Deep South, where people often spoke in riddles and used dichotomies to make a point. It was a land where no one ever truly said what they meant, but were more than happy to gossip behind one's back. John never stood a chance.

The news that he had somehow upset an ADA was deeply troubling to John. Larry, however, didn't expect what was coming. The strangest part of the interaction was Larry's reaction when John and Zack heard that he would be re-testing the substance instead of sending it to the crime lab. Larry had just admitted to tampering with their evidence. It was a brazen move, even for Zack, and a completely foreign concept to John.

The idea that the sanctity of the chain of custody would be violated for a Police Chief's personal ego was absurd. Despite this, John believed it was best not to publicly confront the Police Chief. Instead, he started documenting what had occurred, beginning a running narrative of the events as they unfolded.

John mentally prepared for the day he would have to testify against Larry's actions in court, defending his case and ensuring the suspect's due process. On April 11th, 2022, at around 3:00 pm, John, off duty, received a phone call from Larry. Larry was frantic and spoke nervously. He told John he had re-tested the substance and determined that it was not cocaine. He mentioned he would speak to the District Attorney's office to drop the charges.

Larry hoped John wouldn't protest the flagrant deviation from standard procedures. Then Larry added something damning: he told John that several drug agents from the Worth County Sheriff's Office had assisted him in the test. This raised John's suspicions to new levels. This was too much effort for a simple traffic stop. Larry compounded his mistakes by stressing, emphatically, that John should not tell anyone about the suspected cocaine. Something was clearly wrong, and John was now realizing what Zack had been hinting at—Larry had done something illegal and was trying to cover it up.

John continued documenting everything in his running narrative, realizing that this would be important not just for his case but for the larger implications of Larry's actions. At this point, John knew he would be testifying about the situation. He had no idea, however, how long it would take for the truth to surface—or how much pain and lies Larry would spin over the next few years.

Larry made another critical mistake: he documented the re-test in a simple paragraph report. The report lacked a chain of custody, no images, and no discussion of the test procedure or results, which would have refuted the positive test result images that John had attached to his initial arrest report. While John was prepared to address any questions about the amount of substance in the modified Scott reagent test, he wasn't prepared to explain to other trained officers that they were apparently unable to follow test instructions properly.

Larry unknowingly implicated a conspirator early in the game: Adam Celinski, a cohort of Worth County Sheriff Donald Whitaker. Whether Larry intended to sell the cocaine or keep it for himself, he had help from others in the county who were willing to cover his lie and protect his status, even at the expense of defaming a fellow officer. Zack and John wouldn't realize this until weeks later. Zack, increasingly concerned, shared his worries with John.

On April 13th, 2022, Larry cornered John in a bullying session. Larry didn't mention this conversation to Georgia POST Investigator Douglas Dowdy, but he would omit many things from Dowdy, all while fabricating events that never happened. Larry, playing a role, blamed John for the bond set in the arrested driver's case, despite only judges having the authority to set bonds. The Sheriff and his cohort were integral to this conversation.

Larry further tried to manipulate the situation by claiming that the arrested driver had told him that Worth County deputies had transported her from Turner County Jail to Worth County Jail and had mentioned that John made "bogus charges." Larry also told John that 26 hydrocodone pills weren't enough for a possession charge, let alone a distribution charge (though Georgia's code section was clear on what constituted distribution). Larry also said that Sheriff Don Whitaker "had it in for John" and had ordered Larry to fire him. This statement would prove to be crucial.

Larry completely ignored the driver's prior criminal record in Florida. What John didn't know at the time would become clear later—Larry had already swapped the cocaine for something else. Larry had to act quickly, manipulating John into believing he had made a mistake and that only Larry could help him. This tactic backfired on Larry.

The next day, John went to ADA Sandra Guest, hoping to repair the relationship Larry had claimed was damaged. Guest was confused, unaware of any issues between John and the DA's office. She hadn't even heard about the re-testing or the change in charges. Now, John's suspicions grew. Something was very wrong, and Larry's lies were unraveling.

Zack voiced his concerns to John one night while on duty. John was at home in nearby Sylvester, barely a 10-minute drive from Poulan's police department. Zack had grown so concerned that he removed the case file of the arrest and called John to inform him. John's only thought was to return the case file, but only after scanning and creating PDFs of it for future court reference. The case file now contained no mention of re-testing, no chain of custody changes, or any communications with the District Attorney's office.

John and Zack now expected Larry to lie. John, still new to the complexities of Larry's corruption, was growing more suspicious with each passing day. Zack, more familiar with Larry's reputation, had known what was coming.

Zack brought the case file to John's house, and John scanned it, uploading the digital file to a Google Drive folder he had set up to memorialize everything related to the case. The running narrative, images, test instructions, the chain-of-custody report, the search and seizure report, warrants, probable cause statements, and the original case file were all stored there.

John still believed that he would be testifying to protect his case. He had no idea that his fight would stretch into years of defending his reputation and career as Larry's lies snowballed. Zack, far more aware of what was coming, remained vigilant.

Zack and John did something else Larry didn't expect: they submitted the seized narcotics for crime lab analysis. This simple submission was actually standard procedure in any narcotics-related case. Now, something had to go to the crime lab, and Larry was furious.

On April 18th, 2022, Zack prepared to transport the seized narcotics to the GBI Crime Lab. John had just started his shift. Zack was filling out the chain-of-custody form—a crucial step in the search and seizure process. Larry, in a frenzy, yelled and paced, desperately trying to convince Zack to stop. He spread papers on a table, the same table used for meals, and placed heaps of white powder on sampling strips, screaming, "See! See! It's not cocaine!"

John was dismayed. He knew the weight would now be less than initially reported—one more thing he'd have to explain in court. Zack refused to relent. He secured the evidence, sealed it, and took it to the GBI Crime Lab in Moultrie, Georgia. Larry continued his rant, shouting, "I can't believe you two don't trust me! Do you know what they'll do to me?" John ignored him and went to work. In hindsight, Larry's rant should have been telling, but it would only become clear much later.

When the GBI Crime Lab results came in (after John had to involve a lawyer to retrieve them), they revealed a startling discrepancy. The white powdery substance that had weighed just over 340 grams now "magically" weighed over 460 grams—a difference of over 4 ounces. Neither the GA POST investigator, the FBI, nor the GBI focused on this critical piece of evidence, which clearly showed that Larry Whisenant had tampered with evidence.

This tampering would not only destroy John's career but also allow Larry and Dowdy to publicly brand him as untruthful. It would delay a simple file review for nearly three years, while emboldening Larry to involve command staff from the Oglethorpe County Sheriff's Office, Hartwell Police Department, and high-ranking members of the FBI, GBI, and GA POST—who were all too willing to lie for him and document those lies in official reports and public emails, despite overwhelming audio and written evidence to the contrary.

The substance, originally seized by Watson and Masters, was never definitively identified, as Larry had swapped it with something else entirely.

The positive field test clearly matched the test instructions (pink over blue). The weight of the substance was recorded as 12.18 ounces (approximately 345 grams), and the 26 hydrocodone pills, which the driver had no prescription for, were illegally trafficked across state lines. The substance, however, had changed from a white powder to a solid and now weighed approximately 467 grams—an increase of 122 grams (4.3 ounces). This wasn't a mistake; it was clear evidence of evidence tampering by Larry Whisenant.

No one will ever know what the substance originally seized by Watson and Masters truly was, because Larry Whisenant swapped it with something else.

CHAPTER 4

The Official Lie

Weeks passed since Larry Whisenant's last outburst. He was panicking. Zack and John weren't doing what he expected. They weren't laying down as he had hoped. Larry was frequently seen in Poulan, speaking with Worth County Sheriff's Deputies outside the Poulan Police Department, away from any potential eavesdroppers. The park across from City Hall was his usual spot—an ideal location to spot Zack and John coming and end the conversation abruptly. What Zack and John didn't know was that the Sheriff and his deputies were actively advising Larry on how to get rid of them. The lie was in the process of being created.

Larry had returned the seized items to the arrested driver without informing the case officer. He did this on a weekend when John wasn't on duty, ensuring secrecy. Instead of updating the case file, Larry created an entirely new report number and filed the return of the seized items under that new number. He also had Assistant Chief Frank Walker type up a separate report stating that Zack Watson had returned the seized items, attempting to create discord between Zack and John. Additionally, Larry failed to submit the seizure report and warrants to the District Attorney's Office within the legally required timeframe, using the Chief's report approval process to intentionally delay it past the statutory deadline.

It was the monthly Wednesday meeting on May 4, 2022. Larry and Frank had already left the office. John was performing one of his additional duties, and Zack was preparing to begin his patrol shift. Ironically, it was Frank and Larry's laziness that would eventually expose them. One of John's duties at the Poulan Police Department was sorting and updating case file folders and reporting traffic citation numbers to the Governor's Office of Highway Safety.

Frank and Larry were so arrogant as command staff that after altering the case files and creating two new ones (one of which was falsified), they expected their "subordinates" to file the folders for them. John noticed the two folders immediately among the pile of submitted fingerprint cards and Dispatch CAD (Computer Aided Dispatching) cards. Both folders had the same report number. When he opened them with the intention of combining them, he was horrified by what he found.

One folder contained a chain-of-custody report along with a brief, poorly written narrative that stated Larry Whisenant had returned the arrested driver's belongings. Strangely, the chain-of-custody report indicated that Larry had been in personal possession of the items, even though Zack and John had submitted them to the evidence locker on their chain-of-custody reports. Larry had clearly tampered with evidence—a felony.

The other folder contained a narrative written by Assistant Chief Frank Walker, claiming that Zack Watson—not Larry Whisenant—had returned the items to the arrested driver. Frank's narrative was written as though he had been present for the exchange, but Zack had not been working during that time. Frank had fabricated the statement, another felony. Neither Frank nor Larry were investigated for this serious breach of police procedure. John immediately showed the folders to Zack. Their reactions, however, would differ.

John's response was complex. On one hand, he was angry about the lying, the false reports, and the clear tampering with evidence. On the other hand, he was a well-trained police officer, and his training urged him to push the emotions aside, focusing instead on logic and resilience—traits common in a "natural" police mindset. John wanted to be cautious. His first instinct was to keep documenting the situation, preparing to defend his case in court. He immediately scanned the copies of the reports in the folders and noticed that in the Record Management System (RMS) Poulan Police used, there was a space between a set of numbers, hiding the duplicate report number. John called his FTO from his previous agency for advice, knowing that he would need guidance in the coming days.

Zack's reaction was simpler. Zack had far more experience in law enforcement than John and had learned that in Southwest Georgia, the system would believe whatever Larry said. His experience with law enforcement had shown him widespread corruption and gossip among the ranks. Zack immediately called Larry to confront him. About 20 minutes later, as John was still on the phone with his FTO, there came a loud banging at the side door of the Police Department, as though someone was trying to break it down.

When Zack opened the door, Larry Whisenant stormed into the building, red-faced and screaming. He began an incoherent rant about being the "evidence custodian for the whole damn department!" While John remained silent, Zack attempted to defend his actions and the case. John, however, believed that because Larry was the police chief, no one would take his side against a police chief. Earlier that year, Larry had bragged about the Georgia Association of Chiefs of Police having a secret online forum where Chiefs could talk about rank-and-file officers, even compiling a list of blackballed officers. Larry had warned John not to be mentioned in those forums.

Larry's wild, profanity-laced rant continued, but one statement caught their attention. "Do you think I know her (the arrested driver)?" Larry shouted. "Do you think I fucked her?" Neither John nor Zack had ever suspected that Larry might have engaged in a sexual bribery, but in that moment, Larry's words seemed to confirm it. John and Zack, who saw nothing as random, now recognized this as an honest slip of the tongue.

Larry screamed that the GBI and DA's Office would now be investigating both officers. John believed him. Larry intimated that there would be serious consequences "when" (not if) the GBI and DA took his side.

As Larry's voice eventually wore out, he made another spontaneous remark: "If you guys tell anyone, I'll be put in prison!" John was now fully convinced that Larry had committed illegal acts, at the very least tampering with evidence. Larry's voice eventually grew hoarse from shouting, and John left the room. During the entire exchange, John had said nothing, while Zack and Larry continued their heated conversation. Larry also failed to tell either officer that they had one week to leave the police department, a detail that would become significant later when Larry would tell the Georgia Department of Labor and the Peace Officer Standards and Training Investigator the exact opposite.

The POST Investigator never called to verify these events, choosing instead to fabricate his own version of events, which was also false—an offense in Georgia. Zack stayed behind and later told John that at one point, Larry had nearly broken down in tears, asking what the two officers were going to do next, as though to ask whether John and Zack would report the events.

John believed he was now under investigation by the DA's Office and contacted the Tift Judicial Circuit DA's Office to report the situation. He also called the Police Benevolent Association (PBA) for legal assistance. Although

GA POST did not recognize police labor unions, legal funds were allowed, and John had been paying for PBA assistance since becoming a police officer.

On May 13, 2022, Larry called John. By this point, John had begun recording all conversations using a small handheld recorder typically used by investigators to record interviews. Larry told John, "This isn't working out." John had been at the Poulan Police Department for nearly two years with no disciplinary record. In fact, just a few months earlier, John had received an award from the City Council. To hear that he was no longer performing as required was a shock to him.

Larry handed John a termination letter, dated May 12, 2022, despite letting him work the shift the day before without mentioning anything about the impending termination. John had made traffic stops and made an arrest during that shift, but the letter was dated before those events. John was baffled. Why let him work past the date on the letter and then present it to him the next day? Simply put, Larry didn't know what he was doing.

The letter cited "at-will employment" as the reason for termination.

This would be changed by Larry for the POST Investigator, even though the same Investigator had access to all the documents and audio recordings that proved the termination was illegal and did not warrant any further review. Despite multiple submissions to various members of the Georgia POST chain of command, the official reason for John's termination on his POST record would later read "History of lying to or about the Chief" as of October 2024. Georgia POST not only condoned this behavior but enabled it.

Widely regarded in the community for his lack of effectiveness, Larry Whisenant nonetheless persuaded the City of Poulan to maintain him as Police Chief, despite clear evidence of repeated missteps in his law enforcement duties. He had little knowledge of narcotics and even less of basic traffic law enforcement. He would frequently tell his officers that visual speed estimates were a myth, despite being trained by state standards that visual speed estimates were essential to the use of speed detection devices.

John had only become aware of these facts in the last few weeks, and armed with that knowledge, he had decided to carry a recorder from that point forward. Too many lies, too many secrets. With the recorder, John could easily prove the lies and expose the truth. No more secrets, no more deception. He would keep the recorder in his pocket for the rest of his law enforcement career, always ready to record to ensure everyone remained honest.

The substance that was seized by Watson and Masters in it's original packaging.

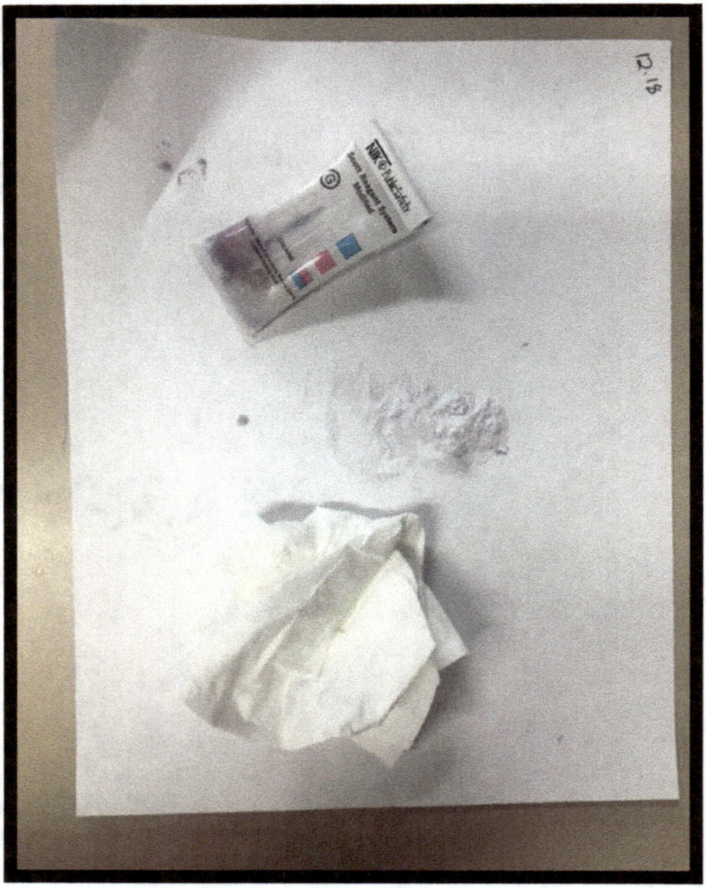

The positive field test kit that clearly matches the test instructions (pink over blue). As the three ampules were broken, they also matched the correct color for the ampules broken in correct succession to arrive at the matching color of pink over blue. Multiple police officers not associated with this case have seen this photo and agree that this is positive filed test for cocaine using a Modified Scott Reagent field test kit. Take note of the weight, in ounces, in the top left hand corner 12.18 ounces (approximately 345 grams).

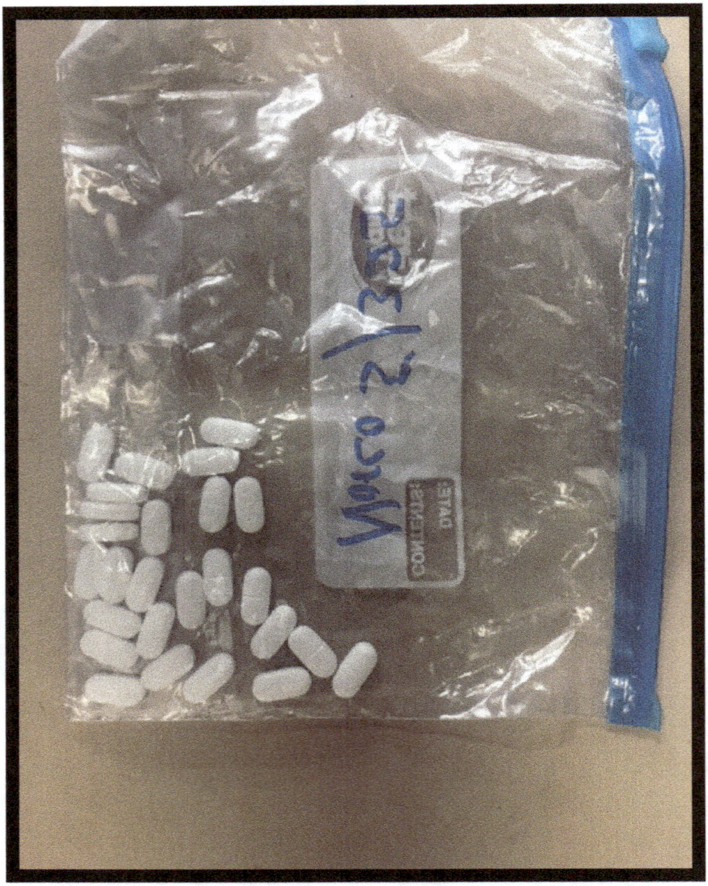

The 26 "norco" pills that the driver did not have a prescription for and that she admitted she had trafficked across state lines after illegally acquiring them.

Official Report

Division of Forensic Sciences
Georgia Bureau of Investigation
State of Georgia

Southwestern Regional Lab
DOFS Case #: 2022-5001116
Report Date: 06/23/2022

Cleveland Miles
Deputy Director

ANAB Accredited ISO/IEC 17025
Testing Laboratory

Requested Service: Drug identification
Agency: Poulan Police Department
Agency Ref#: 22197
Requested by: J. Masters

Case Individuals:
Subject: [redacted]

Evidence

On 04/16/2022, the laboratory received the following evidence from the Poulan Police Department via Lockbox

2022-5001116-001	Sealed package(s) containing the following
2022-5001116-001A	one bag of solid material
2022-5001116-001B	one bag with tablets [M365]

Examinations Performed:

Evidence Submission #001A
- Electronic balance and/or mechanical scale
- Gas chromatography/Mass spectrometry
- High Performance Liquid Chromatography
- Ultraviolet spectroscopy

Evidence Submission #001B
- Electronic balance and/or mechanical scale
- Gas chromatography/Mass spectrometry
- Logo Identification

Results and Conclusions

Evidence Submission #001A
No controlled substances confirmed in the sample tested as defined by O.C.G.A. § 16-13
Net weight of sample tested: 467.458 gram(s) +/- 0.007 gram(s)

Evidence Submission #001B
Analysis confirms the presence of hydrocodone in the sample tested. Schedule II
Tested 1 tablet
Net weight of total sample: 10.345 gram(s) +/- 0.004 gram(s)

Measurement Uncertainty:
Estimations of measurement uncertainty for all quantitative determinations in Drug Identification are reported at a coverage probability of 99.73%.

Only those items discussed in the results above were analyzed for this report. The above represents the interpretations/opinions of the undersigned analyst. Unless noted above, evidence analyzed in this report will be returned to the submitting agency. Biological evidence (body fluids and tissues) and proof determination evidence will be destroyed after one year. This report may not be reproduced except in full without written permission of the laboratory.

Technical notes and data supporting the conclusions and findings in this report are maintained within the laboratory case records.

This case may contain evidence that must be preserved in accordance with O.C.G.A. § 17-5-56

Report Date: 06/23/2022
Report id: 8NHWL6BD0S1T43
Template Rev: 2015-12-11

Page 1 of 2

Note the substance had changed from white powdery to a "solid" substance and now weighed approx. 467 grams; a difference of 122 grams (4.3 ounces). That is not accidental; but a profound, black and white, surety of tampering with evidence by Larry Whisenant. No one will ever know what the substance that was seized by Watson and Masters is, because clearly Larry Whisenant swapped it with something else.

Mayor
Robert Greer

City Clerk
Diana Harris

City of Poulan
204 N Hunton Street
P.O. Box 69
Poulan, Georgia 31781

229-776-4097/Telephone 229-776-2998/Fax

May 12, 2022

John Masters

Dear Mr. Masters:

Pursuant to Article 8 of the Personnel Policies and Procedures for the City of Poulan, you are being dismissed from your position as a police officer with the City. The effective date of your dismissal is May 27, 2022. You are being placed on administrative leave until that time. You are expected to surrender all equipment in your possession belonging to the City of Poulan including but not limited to uniforms, weapons, and all other equipment issued to you. Your dismissal is a proposed action. However, it will become final if you fail to respond and request an appeal from the City Clerk within five (5) business days. Failure to respond will result in the loss of an opportunity to appeal your dismissal and your dismissal will be implemented as proposed in this letter. The hearing will be before the Mayor and City Council.

The City of Poulan is an "at-will" employer. The hearing provided under the personnel policies does not alter you're at-will status or create any property interest in your employment with the City. The City is not required to give the causes for discipline action either in the City's Personnel Policy or at the time of any adverse action, the City is not required to dismiss for so called "just cause".

Your conduct should be governed according to this letter.

Sincerely,

Larry Whisenant

The letter served to Masters by Whisenant personally.

Mayor
Robert Greer

City Clerk
Jennifer Sheler

City of Poulan
204 N Hunton Street
P.O. Box 69
Poulan, Georgia 31781

229-776-4097/Telephone 229-776-2998/Fax

June 30, 2022

Mr. John Masters

Dear Mr. Masters:

The matter of your hearing from your appeal of your termination from the employment with the City of Poulan came before the Mayor and City Council on June 28, 2022. After careful consideration of the evidence you presented, the Mayor and Council have voted unanimously to affirm your termination as a police officer for the City of Poulan.

The City regrets the necessity to take this action.

Sincerely,

Robert Greer, Mayor

cc Charles Cox

The letter mailed to Masters by the Mayor at the conclusion of the appeal hearing

CHAPTER 5

The Lie Transforms...

The Georgia Peace Officer Standards and Training Council (POST) is the governing body that oversees all peace officer certifications in the state of Georgia. According to their mission statement, POST "provides the citizens of Georgia with qualified, professionally trained, ethical, and competent peace officers and criminal justice professionals." POST has rules that both agencies and POST itself are supposed to follow. Except, in this case, apparently, they didn't.

The intent behind POST's oversight is to ensure that the truth is revealed whenever any certified officer (regardless of rank) engages in compromising, incompetent, or illegal behavior. In John's case, however, this did not occur—not by a long shot. Not only did the GA POST Investigator promise Larry Whisenant a specific outcome, but he also did everything he could (including making outright false statements, which is a felony) to bring that promised outcome to fruition. It would seem strange to the average person that a POST Investigator would go to such lengths, but the answer is simple: the assigned GA POST Investigator was the retired Tifton Police Chief, and he was friends with Larry Whisenant.

Larry often boasted about the influential friends he had in the Georgia Association of Chiefs of Police (GACP) and the GA POST Council. He would threaten officers with "blackballing" from the GACP "club" if they didn't obey his demands, such as meeting the citation quotas or other expectations he set. Many believed him. If officers left Poulan Police with Larry upset at them, they knew they would never be able to return to law enforcement in Georgia. One man exerting such control is inherently dangerous; however, John and Zack didn't buy it.

John was fully prepared to challenge Larry's 'good ol' boy' network with the growing evidence that was rapidly accumulating.

John filed an appeal with the City of Poulan, catching them off guard. The city council had to reschedule the appeal hearing because they didn't know how to conduct one. Due process and the speedy appeal process outlined in the city policy manual were thrown out the window, along with the city's progressive discipline policy. The city also placed John on administrative leave but refused to pay him. When John filed for unemployment, the City of Poulan lied to the Georgia Department of Labor, stating that John was employed full-time and receiving pay. Tampering with evidence had now turned into forgery of federal and state documents. This would not be the last time.

Before the appeal, Frank Walker made several attempts to get John to accept a voluntary resignation. He began texting one of the city's volunteer firefighters, describing what had supposedly happened. The firefighter shared the texts with John, who kept them for future reference. Frank told the firefighter that he (Frank) had been in the room during the confrontation with Larry, not Zack. He also said that John had called Larry that night and accused him of something. The firefighter, a friend of John's, was being used in an attempt to sway John's appeal before the hearing. They needed to know what was going to be said during the hearing. Meanwhile, Larry began inventing fictitious "write-ups" and adding them to John's personnel file. John had never signed these write-ups because he had no knowledge of them or the policy violations they supposedly documented. At least one of the write-ups was dated nearly three months before John even started working at the City of Poulan.

One mistake Larry made with the fabricated write-ups was claiming that John had sought employment with Pelham Police and had told Larry about it. The problem with Larry's story was that Zack Watson worked at Pelham Police and was in contact with their command staff. Zack had told Larry about a bonus offer Pelham Police was using to attract certified officers. When John overheard Zack mention this at one of the monthly meetings, he interpreted it as Zack asking Larry if Poulan should implement a similar incentive to attract certified officers. But now, Larry was twisting this conversation into one John never had. Larry also made sure to remove any awards or accolades John had received from the official personnel file.

Frank sent the firefighter more absurd texts about John, even accusing him of being a Satanist. Larry began telling people that John had quit, not been fired. John heard this from Public Works employees at the county dump (another conversation he recorded). Larry also spread a rumor in the community that John had masturbated in a patrol car. When those same people spoke to Zack, they learned it was a completely false rumor.

Frank told John he was going to talk to Turner County Sheriff Andy Hester, who was also a member of the GA POST Council. Frank pretended to John that he knew Hester and suggested that Hester could help John find a job if he submitted a voluntary resignation. Frank and Larry needed a voluntary resignation. It was important that there was no attention drawn to the termination or the inevitable aftermath. John refused the bribe.

There were many threats and insinuations while John awaited his appeal hearing. John's PBA dues entitled him to an attorney to assist during the appeal. On the night of the appeal hearing, despite prior notice, neither Frank Walker nor Larry Whisenant showed up. They knew the lawyer had seen the documentation that John had been compiling and didn't want to be questioned about it.

At the start of the hearing, the city attorney, Tommy Coleman, reminded the city council that they didn't have to follow city policy because Georgia is a right-to-work state; they could terminate anyone at any time, without cause. This statement guaranteed the City of Poulan would face a lawsuit if they followed through with Coleman's advice. Tommy Coleman was a failed mayor of Albany, Georgia, and now made a living giving bad advice to small cities throughout southwest Georgia.

Despite the proven evidence that Larry had tampered with evidence and that Frank had assisted in writing false reports to cover it up, the

City Council unanimously voted to terminate John. None of this information seemed to resonate with the city council or the lawyer who was supposed to advise them. Any other city in America would have immediately called for an independent investigation, but not Poulan. They claimed to know everything and went so far as to tell people in the community that John would have his peace officer certification revoked by GA POST.

The city did record, for the record, during John's appeal that there was no discipline on file and confirmed that they were terminating him for "at-will employment." This fact would be reiterated by journalists who came years later with questions. Despite this "no discipline" confirmation from Frank Walker and multiple members of the Poulan City Council, Coleman and Larry would direct false discipline to both the Georgia Department of Labor and the assigned GA POST Investigator, changing the story and reasons for termination not just once, but three times on official government documents. That is a crime—a felony in the state of Georgia.

The city followed up with a letter sent to John's home after the hearing, confirming the "at-will employment" termination. The letter stated that the council "regretted" the decision. Despite this official correspondence, the GA POST Investigator happily took the false statements Larry had fabricated, along with a few of his own after a recorded interview with John, and turned them into nearly 10 pages of rambling, fantastical storytelling in an attempt to defame John and revoke his certification, as had been promised. Douglas Dowdy, like Larry Whisenant, could not leave this to chance. John Masters had to be removed from law enforcement at any cost.

Another disturbing fact is that Larry Whisenant never gave POST the official reason for John's termination. POST clearly never received the letter from the Chief or the second letter from the City Council confirming the "at-will employment" termination. At least not from the City of Poulan or from Larry Whisenant. Such a letter would have invalidated the need for any POST investigation, and Larry knew that. Intentionally withholding relevant information from a GA POST Investigator is not only a violation of the GA POST Act, but a criminal offense in Georgia, as it violates the oath of office —a felony.

Nevertheless, it was in Poulan's best interest to manufacture other reasons for John's termination, especially after he sued the city for wrongful termination. Clearly, the City of Poulan and Larry Whisenant were involved in criminal activity and at risk of being exposed. They had no choice but to lie. They couldn't admit to the POST Council that Larry had tampered with evidence, and that they were either complicit or willing to ignore it.

John had found another agency to work for while under File Review, but Larry wasn't going to leave anything to chance. Larry spoke to Oglethorpe County Sheriff's Office Chief Deputy Jason Taft during the lawsuit proceedings. Taft openly told John to quit or be fired, and then he micromanaged John's exit from Oglethorpe County. Prior to this meeting, John had been performing well at Oglethorpe County Sheriff's Office. He had written and was managing a car seat grant for the Department of Public Health and had even applied to be the GOHS Traffic

Enforcement Network Assistant Coordinator. He was denied the position due to a "reputation" in South Georgia—Larry's work again. Four weeks later, Taft would be getting rid of John after that conversation with Larry.

Larry had apparently not warned Taft about John's new recording technique, so the events at Oglethorpe County Sheriff's Office were well-documented and would be uploaded to the same Google Drive John maintained. Taft even went so far as to call John after he had agreed to leave, telling him his resignation was not to his standards and instructing him to rewrite it using another deputy's resignation as a template. John complied, fully aware that the unlawful orders were being recorded. The GA POST Investigator would never include this in his notes, another criminal omission.

John's last day at Oglethorpe County, according to the resignation letter and Oglethorpe County Human Resources, was 09/23/2023. However, Taft updated GA POST to show that John had left on 08/19/2023, two days before Taft had even told John to "quit or be fired" on 08/21/2023. Once again, Larry was advising people incorrectly, and these events were being dated prior to their actual occurrence. But Larry had done this before, and so far it had worked. GA POST was buying Larry's lies, so why wouldn't other people?

John tried one last department, Hartwell Police. Larry followed him there as well. John's direct supervisor, Paul Agnew, told him that he had performed his own background check on John and knew "everything" about him. Agnew also said he was going to "drum him out of law enforcement." He started a series of vicious rumors about John, including telling the Assistant Police Chief in an email that John had lied about his military service while alone with Agnew's wife —an event that never happened. John left Hartwell in less than four months, exhausted by the continuous culture of lying among supervisors and command staff in Georgia law enforcement.

The final straw came when Agnew told a dispatcher that John had pointed his weapon at him. The dispatcher informed John, and once again, John was recording the conversation. Unfortunately for Oglethorpe County and Hartwell Police, when Douglas Dowdy called, these same rumors and innuendo were placed in John's POST investigation notes, something they probably didn't know John would later see at the end of the File Review. GA POST would spend much of 2024 blundering through multiple lies from two different directors, including lying to other states during background checks to avoid telling them about the File Review.

All of these events were uploaded to John's Google Drive, which the GA POST investigator had complete access to. Instead of comparing his own notes to actual documentation and recorded conversations, the GA POST Investigator chose to lie for his friend Larry Whisenant. Such easily proven false statements, when the POST Investigator had access to documentation disproving them, can only mean one thing: the POST Investigator either ignored the documentation on purpose or, more likely, did so out of incompetence.

Larry Whisenant had not warned anyone about John's documentation and audio recording. They were all doomed to fail and take the fall for Larry's lies and tampering. Larry knew that, and now he hoped that if he got enough high-ranking people involved with him, they would collectively be too big to arrest—or at least, they would take more punishment than he did. Larry was using everyone around him, and they didn't even know it. His hope was that if enough people were dirty with him, they would be forced to cover him and themselves.

CHAPTER 6

Of Federal Agents, Mice, and Men...

While John was working at Oglethorpe County, an FBI agent in Georgia named Tim Armentrout had heard about the evidence tampering by Larry Whisenant from a confidential source. The source was the same former FTO of John, who had witnessed the entire confrontation between Zack and Larry. The source also knew that John had documented the entire event and its aftermath. Armentrout needed more, though—he wanted to hear it directly from John. When John's former FTO told him about this, he became instantly nervous.

John had spent time overseas in the US Army, serving in Iraq and Afghanistan, among other countries. His foreign service had exposed him to the FBI, the State Department, and other government agencies. John had personal feelings about federal law enforcement; he didn't consider them to be real police officers, not even under a broad definition. He still believed in the righteous mission of the Department of Justice, despite the fact that many field agents lacked actual street cop experience. To John, federal law enforcement was more of a domestic intelligence service rather than true law enforcement. Having arrest powers didn't automatically make an agent a cop.

John knew to be cautious when dealing with any FBI agent. He had previously interacted with off-duty FBI and ATF agents during traffic stops. They flashed their badges, and on one occasion, an agent even pulled out a gun while sitting in his vehicle during a stop. John handled it patiently, assuming the agent was poorly trained, which turned out to be true once his credentials were confirmed.

John saw these agents as brash and dismissive of local and state law enforcement.

They acted as if they were superior and often treated local officers with disdain. From John's experience, federal agents never had to follow traffic laws or state codes, including impaired driving statutes. John was as formally educated as many federal agents, and he had more life experience, but their condescending attitude toward local police was unmistakable.

John didn't want to interact with Armentrout, but his sense of loyalty to the government, which was unusual compared to most Americans, outweighed his personal reservations. He believed that the federal government had just as much right to enforce laws and protect national interests as the states did, through domestic intelligence services like the FBI. However, John held a constructionist view of the Constitution, and these two perspectives often conflicted. His family had immigrated to the United States, and they had been treated well by the country, both economically and physically. They had performed military service to achieve citizenship, and the generations that followed had continued this legacy of public service. John felt a deep loyalty to the United States, which led him to believe that he should cooperate with federal law enforcement, regardless of his personal feelings or their motives.

John decided that he would cooperate with the FBI, but only with legal counsel present. When he expressed this, Armentrout appeared to hesitate. During a phone call, Armentrout told John that despite reviewing the evidence and assuring him he had done nothing wrong, there would be no federal investigation into Larry Whisenant.

Larry now had a green light to start a campaign against John. Armentrout's refusal to pursue a case meant that Larry could tell people that the FBI had "cleared" him, thus justifying his attack on John's career.

The next step was to involve a high-ranking GBI agent. If things went wrong, Larry could claim that the GBI had cleared him through an investigation. Larry only revealed a small portion of the truth to Kim Baker, the GBI Special Agent in Charge of Region 15. Dowdy later referenced this contact in his investigative notes, using it as Larry had intended. According to Dowdy, Larry had done nothing illegal, based on information he received from GBI SAC Kim Baker. Whether she had actually been told anything about the incident would probably never be known, but her statement made it official. Larry now had an official state document that cleared him of wrongdoing by the Georgia Bureau of Investigation.

After John left the Hartwell Police Department, the City of Poulan settled out of court for wrongful termination. They paid John a small sum to cover damages and sent a letter to GA POST requesting that John's departure be recorded as a "Voluntary Resignation" rather than "Termination." Poulan wanted to distance itself from Larry's mistakes and avoid whatever consequences were sure to follow. GA POST amended the record, which shocked multiple officers, as such public statements were unheard of. This letter was conveniently omitted from Dowdy's investigative notes, another criminal omission. A pattern was forming between Larry Whisenant and Douglas Dowdy.

According to Dowdy's report, he had supposedly spoken with John at length about the stop and the events that followed. However, this alleged conversation never occurred. Larry had failed to inform Dowdy about John's recording and documentation of the incident. In reality, Dowdy had only had a brief conversation with John, during which the termination wasn't discussed. Dowdy spent most of the time telling John that his certification was likely to be revoked, suspended, or placed on probation, and discussed the GA POST protocols for investigations and sanctions. Dowdy also confirmed that no investigation would be conducted into the actions of the Poulan Police Chief or the termination. John had recorded the entire conversation, uploading it to the Google Drive he was maintaining. Dowdy had full access to this information. Clearly, it was no longer ignorance but incompetence that influenced Dowdy's decisions.

Dowdy had previously contacted Zackery Watson, who provided Dowdy with a copy of the Google Drive containing all the information and recordings John had kept, including narratives and audio. Dowdy referred to it as a "diary," treating John as a child rather than a professional officer. This was not mentioned in Dowdy's investigative notes, another criminal omission. Dowdy's opinion was written into a jumbled, nonsensical narrative that followed no logical order. By Dowdy's own admission, the report lacked evidence, despite his attempts to obtain or fabricate it from official sources.

None of the 10-page report contained any proof that John had made false statements, as Dowdy had accused. It read like a work of fiction, blending elements of Agatha Christie, Tom Clancy, and Ray Bradbury—entertaining but utterly inappropriate for an official government document.

The problem with Dowdy's report was that "making untruthful statements" was not the reason for John's termination by the Poulan Police Department. Poulan had documented multiple times that there were no policy violations or disciplinary actions at the time of John's termination. This was confirmed in the paperwork provided to John. Changing the reason for termination after the fact—especially after a lawsuit had been filed—meant that Larry had either lied to Dowdy or involved him directly in the tampering. Based on Dowdy's own words, it was clear that Dowdy was directly complicit in the cover-up orchestrated by Larry Whisenant.

Dowdy's report came after John had conducted several interviews with a podcaster and an Atlanta-based investigative journalist about the events at the Poulan Police Department. One interview revealed that GA POST had sent a letter of good standing to another state, despite John being under "File Review." This seemed like an attempt to get John out of Georgia, but when the other state found out about the File Review, they stopped the hiring process. Two GA POST division directors had also given John conflicting timelines and results regarding his File Review. Dowdy had everyone running in circles. No one knew who to trust.

These interviews also detailed the circumstances surrounding Poulan's citation quotas, Larry's criminal activities, and the City of Poulan's failure to investigate Larry. The death threats directed at John by officers from other agencies on Larry's behalf were also discussed.

This led to backlash against John and Zack. John was warned that if he didn't stop, he would never be allowed to be a police officer again. John internally laughed at this empty threat. He was already no longer a police officer; what else could they do to him? If they were going to take action, they would have done it by now.

The investigative notes were sent in a letter after the Probable Cause Committee hearing. GA POST foolishly sent the letter to an attorney hired by the PBA to represent John. However, John had stopped paying his dues, fired the attorney, and formally removed himself from the PBA months before the hearing. Both Poulan and GA POST investigators knew this.

That attorney forwarded the letter, along with Dowdy's rambling, fantastical story that defamed John. It became public record. John shared the letter with Zackery Watson, who then shared it with others, including the Atlanta-based journalist who had previously interviewed them. The journalist did a follow-up report, revealing that GA POST, despite Dowdy's statement, had chosen "No Action" on John's File Review. GA POST wanted to distance itself from Larry and Dowdy's lies, hoping that the "No Action" would stop further interviews or documentation. As of the publication of this book, the 10-page document had still not been uploaded to John's POST record.

Larry Whisenant, Frank Walker, and Douglas Dowdy were now documented liars. Whether Dowdy and Frank helped Larry cover up his actions, or whether they were complicit in the lies and official documentation meant to destroy an honest officer, remained unclear. But one thing was certain: no investigation had been conducted into the actions of Larry Whisenant, Frank Walker, or Douglas Dowdy.

CHAPTER 7

"Buddy"

Douglas "Buddy" Dowdy is a man full of contradictions. The retired police chief of Tifton, GA, presents himself as a devoted family man and a religious, God-fearing individual. The reality, however, could not be further from the truth. He is a small-minded, petty, and hard-hearted person; it's difficult to understand how he ever became a police officer, let alone a Police Chief and a GA POST investigator.

Before assuming his position at GA POST, Dowdy had retired from the City of Tifton and was working as a regular patrol officer at Abraham Baldwin Agricultural College Police

Department. This was a significant step down from his supposedly long and honorable career as the City of Tifton's top cop. It would be safe to say that, once again, local law enforcement in the area knew things that others outside of Southwest Georgia did not know—similar to Whisenant.

John recalled seeing Dowdy while he was being trained at the Georgia Public Safety Training Center Regional Academy in Tifton, located on the ABAC college grounds. Dowdy had appeared sullen, and would remain there working at ABAC Police until the death of Jimmy Callaway. Callaway, the Director of the GA POST Investigative Division, had been contacted by John regarding the events at Poulan Police and his termination while on unpaid administrative leave. Later that August, Callaway passed away suddenly from natural causes in a Savannah hotel room.

Callaway's death brought internal changes at GA POST that would greatly benefit Whisenant. A spot opened up for Dowdy to become the District Investigator. However, it soon became clear that, like the rest of his time in law enforcement, Dowdy really had no idea what he was doing. A bumbling buffoon, his disregard for rules and policy made one wonder if he had ever done his job to any legal standard.

After managing to secure a position at GA POST as an investigator, one of Dowdy's first cases was John Masters' termination from Poulan. Dowdy and Whisenant were friends, and Dowdy had been known to discuss local officers with Whisenant. Masters had lived in Tifton before moving to Sylvester for work. When Masters spoke with the Tift County Sheriff's Office about one of his cases involving them, Whisenant erupted, accusing Masters of attempting to switch to the Tift County Sheriff's Office. Masters had not applied, but Whisenant screamed at him about "disloyalty," citing information allegedly given to him by the Tifton Police Chief—none of which was true.

Dowdy's handling of the Masters investigation was lazy, at best. He contacted only one other person involved in the case, Zackery Watson. According to Dowdy, it was an extensive and exhaustive interview, but Watson described it as brief and lasting less than five minutes. During this interaction, Watson had given Dowdy full access to the Google Drive Masters had been keeping. Dowdy refused to contact the other witness to Whisenant's rant or any other individuals involved. There is no explanation in Dowdy's notes as to why he failed to contact the other witness. Another criminal omission.

For reasons unknown, Dowdy decided to contact individuals who were not connected to the termination at Poulan in any way—at least, not in a manner Dowdy would have known. This is a telling sign. The proof that Whisenant had contacted the Oglethorpe County Sheriff's Office and Hartwell Police Department is in Dowdy's investigation. Dowdy was aware to call these agencies because Jason Taft and Paul Agnew had admitted to speaking with Whisenant. Dowdy confirmed this in his 10-page "fantasy novel" and made the connection between Whisenant and Oglethorpe County Sheriff's Office and Hartwell Police. There was no other reason to contact these agencies unless Whisenant had instructed Dowdy to do so. Dowdy's blundering confirmed the collusion he was attempting to cover up.

Hartwell's statement to Dowdy reads like something from a bad spy novel. It included emails from Sergeant Paul Agnew to Assistant Chief Stan Sayer, where the sergeant admitted to being instructed to write the emails—which would undoubtedly include their contents. Dowdy based his investigative assertions about Masters on information from an agency head, who got his information from his assistant chief, who got his information from Agnew's emails. Essentially, Dowdy was incorporating hearsay into official state documents, which is both irresponsible and unethical. The problem is, Dowdy's investigative notes were official government documents, and any lies within them were grounds for criminal charges and arrest.

The basic allegations had also shifted again. It now read, "History of Lying to or about the Chief." Unfortunately for Dowdy, the 10 pages contained no evidence of lying. In fact, it showed no proof of any investigation into the events that led to Masters' termination from the City of Poulan. All it demonstrated was hearsay, taken from the words that others had been instructed to write by Dowdy. Here's the twist: The City of Poulan had already sent a letter to GA POST changing the termination to a Voluntary

Resignation. If John had voluntarily resigned from Poulan, there would have been no need for a File Review. Poulan had also, on multiple occasions, confirmed to news media, journalists, and lawyers via official documentation that there were no disciplinary issues with John while serving at the Poulan Police Department.

Poulan knew their Chief had lied and committed several felonies. They needed the investigation to end, and they were counting on POST to pick up the hint. But POST didn't. Dowdy stated as much in his 10-page "romance novel" with Whisenant. Dowdy claimed to have had continuous contact with Whisenant and followed his directions—contacts that were dated after the letter was sent. Dowdy had, presumably, promised Whisenant a favorable outcome and was not picking up on the hint that the City of Poulan was trying to send to POST: "Please stop, Masters has evidence that the City of Poulan broke the law."

Buddy also made a damning admission. He confessed that Whisenant had told him that he had stopped the substance from going to the crime lab and intercepted it without performing proper chain of custody. That statement alone proves Whisenant committed a felony—tampering with evidence.

Dowdy would compile all this into his 10-page keyboard incontinence, proving once and for all to the public that he was unfit to even take a patrol report, let alone serve in any capacity of law enforcement. His report read like a hastily assembled romance novel mixed with a murder mystery and spy thriller. Dowdy used official-sounding words and phrases to bind his sloppy investigation, which violated nearly every rule GA POST has for its investigations. None of it could be proven true, but it made for an entertaining read. A copy of the 10 pages of "Notice of P.O.S.T. Discipline" is included in the appendix of this book.

CHAPTER 8

Georgia Peace Officer Standards and Training

Despite the severe accusations written in Dowdy's report, the Georgia POST (Peace Officer Standards and Training) Council clearly recognized them as either a fabrication at worst or a public embarrassment at best. They ultimately chose to take "No Action" regarding Masters' certification. This decision is significant, as it shows that even the POST Council did not support Dowdy's investigation as being truthful. Had any of the 10 pages that Dowdy had painstakingly invented been true and provable, POST would have taken disciplinary action against Masters—at least by placing him on probation, if not suspending or revoking his certification.

Dowdy claimed that his so-called "evidence" showed definitive proof (despite the contrary evidence he repeatedly omitted) that Masters had violated several provisions of the Official Code of Georgia Annotated 35-8-7.1 (a)(2), (a)(6), (a)(7), and (a)(11). POST acknowledged that Dowdy had supposedly proven this, yet chose not to revoke Masters' certification. This is telling. The alleged violations were serious enough to warrant revocation, but POST chose to ignore them, knowing full well that Dowdy's allegations were fabricated.

2024 CODE OF GEORGIA

Title 35 - LAW ENFORCEMENT OFFICERS AND AGENCIES

Chapter 8 - EMPLOYMENT AND TRAINING OF PEACE OFFICERS

Section 35-8-7.1 - Authority of council to refuse certificate to applicant or to discipline council-certified officers; grounds for restoration of certificate; emergency suspension of certification; notice of investigation; retention of records

(a) The council has the authority to refuse certification to an applicant or discipline a council-certified officer or exempt officer under this chapter or any prior law if the council determines that the officer or applicant:

1. Failed to demonstrate the qualifications or standards for certification as set forth in this chapter or the rules and regulations of the council.
2. Knowingly made misleading, deceptive, untrue, or fraudulent representations in the practice of being an officer or in any related document, or practiced fraud or deceit, or made false statements to obtain certification.
3. Has been convicted of a felony in this state, another state, or any jurisdiction, including federal law.
4. Committed a crime involving moral turpitude, regardless of conviction.
5. Had their certificate or license revoked, suspended, annulled, or disciplined by any lawful certifying authority.

6. Engaged in unprofessional, unethical, deceptive, or harmful conduct, even if no actual injury resulted.

7. Violated or attempted to violate any law, rule, or regulation that governs officer conduct, whether criminally punishable or not.

8. Committed an act or omission showing bad moral character or untrustworthiness.

9. Was deemed mentally incompetent by a court of law.

10. Became unable to perform duties due to illness, substance use, or any mental or physical condition.

11. Was suspended or discharged from their law enforcement position for disciplinary reasons.

Section (a)(11) is particularly revealing. It claims there was discipline related to John's termination by the City of Poulan. However, no such discipline was ever presented by Poulan. In fact, multiple recordings and written statements from Poulan officials confirm that no disciplinary action was taken while John was employed there.

This was publicly confirmed during a news interview with John and Watson, where Poulan admitted there had been no discipline during John's time with the department, a fact broadcast internationally.

Dowdy's investigation had put Georgia POST in a difficult position: either Dowdy lied, or Whisenant lied. Either way, someone had lied, and it was not John or Zackery. When John attempted to leave the state and continue working in law enforcement elsewhere, GA POST Certification Director Terry McCormick filled out a letter stating that John was certifiable as a peace officer, without mentioning the "File Review." However, John was honest, and when the state in question learned of the File Review, they halted the hiring process.

GA POST never officially notified John of any hearing regarding the File Review. Instead, they sent this information to an attorney John had previously retained for the appeal with the City of Poulan, and later dismissed. He had hired another attorney for the wrongful termination lawsuit against the City, but POST never sent that attorney anything. This left John in the dark about the hearing process, and it appeared intentional.

POST only violated their own procedural rules if they had a reason to prevent John from speaking publicly. They had read Dowdy's 10 pages and John's written statement and were well aware of the multiple witnesses to Whisenant's criminal activity. It was better for POST to call John a liar, prevent him from participating in the public hearing, and quietly end the File Review.

John did not comply with POST's expectations. He was dissatisfied with the way the File Review ended, especially with his POST record falsely stating a "History of lying to or about the chief." John had not lied—others had. The first edition of this book was written as a public response to Dowdy's investigative report because no legal mechanism had allowed John to challenge POST's actions. There was no question that John intended to speak out against Dowdy and Whisenant in his own defense.

The first hearing notice came from the investigative division, and John did not want to have a hearing with the probable cause committee. His intention was to present the matter, and the evidence, before the full POST Council. However, he was never served with a second hearing notice. When he emailed POST, he received an uncertified letter stating that the Council had no intention of hearing from him. This letter was signed by POST Council member Steve Hyman, the Tifton Police Chief, raising the possibility that Dowdy now had influence over Council members.

This was telling. POST did not want to discipline John despite the serious accusations. They couldn't prove any of Dowdy's fabricated story, and they knew John had numerous witnesses and concrete evidence that Whisenant and Walker had committed multiple felonies, in addition to proof of Dowdy's false statements. POST needed the issue to disappear, but John wasn't going away.

POST had the power to resolve the issue with minimal fallout. All they had to do was ensure the termination reason from Whisenant and the City Attorney aligned with John's POST record. Instead, they chose to retain Dowdy's fabricated reason for termination. Masters was never allowed to see the paperwork that Whisenant sent to Dowdy, but clearly, Whisenant had altered the termination reason. Dowdy and Whisenant were friends, and GA POST failed to protect themselves from the consequences of their reckless actions.

When John pointed this out to GA POST, they responded by saying the City of Poulan directly informed them of the allegation of "History of lying to or about the chief." They told John that unless he had a letter from the City stating otherwise (despite having received such a letter from the City Attorney), GA POST would continue to publicly accuse John of this. This, despite clear evidence to the contrary and no proof of the allegations made by Dowdy. POST chose to continue with the false narrative.

GA POST acted in the knowledge that police officers in Georgia have no real ability to defend themselves against the unchecked power of the POST Council. The POST Council knew that there would be no repercussions for their actions.

CHAPTER 9

Corruption

June 1971 was a significant month in world history. Vietnam Veterans for a Just Peace held a public event to protest the ongoing conflict. Heavy fighting continued around Khe Sanh, where PAVN (North Vietnamese) troops gradually pushed against South Vietnamese Marines stationed at firebases in the area. Jimmy Hoffa announced from prison that he would not run for re-election as Teamsters president. Soviet cosmonauts Vladislav Volkov, Georgi Dobrovolski, and Viktor Patsayev tragically died in the Soyuz 11 disaster. The film *Willy Wonka and the Chocolate*

Factory, starring Gene Wilder, was released in theaters.

On June 17, 1971, U.S. President Richard Nixon declared that "public enemy number one is drug abuse," acknowledging the growing epidemic of overdose deaths that had been occurring since the 1880s. By 1973, the Drug Enforcement Administration (DEA) would be created.

While the DEA's effectiveness has been widely debated by experts, there is no denying the devastation caused by narcotics-related abuse in the United States, which dates back to the first opioid epidemic of the 1880s. The biggest challenge for street-level law enforcement, however, is not the drugs themselves but the corruption the drug trade brings to the countries it poisons.

Law enforcement has always been at a disadvantage in the so-called War on Drugs. Honest officers lack the financial resources to maintain integrity when facing police commanders and fellow officers who are susceptible to the lure of the multi-trillion-dollar drug profits. Against dishonest, corrupt officers, the honest ones stand no chance. In the early

1900s, one of the most common forms of police corruption in the United States was through bribery.

Larry Whisenant, and others like him, have shown that little has changed since the turn of the 20th century. On March 14, 2024, Henry Chapman, a Charlotte-Mecklenburg police officer, was caught on body camera stealing nearly $1,000 from a suspect who had been arrested for an outstanding warrant. Though this was the first time the officer was caught, it was undoubtedly not the first time he had done it.

In 2017, all of the members of the Baltimore Police Department's Gun Trace Task Force were indicted for racketeering and other criminal offenses, including stealing from suspects, planting evidence, and conducting illegal searches and seizures. While multiple victims came forward, only a few of their cases progressed to charges against the former officers. Again, this was not the first time these officers had committed such acts—it was merely the first time they had been caught.

In the late 1990s and early 2000s, about seventy members of the LAPD's CRASH antigang unit were indicted for various corruption schemes, including false arrests, unprovoked use of force, narcotics distribution, and covering up these offenses. Known as the Rampart Scandal (named after the Rampart Division of the LAPD), this scandal continues to shape Los Angeles politics to this day. It also led to significant changes in LAPD policies. As the public learned more, it was revealed that a culture of stealing and distributing narcotics had existed among many officers within the department.

In the 21st century, many members of the public believe in a "blue line" of silence among police officers. Those not involved will not "rat out" or expose those engaging in illegal activities. This is especially true among command staff, particularly in states where no union representation exists to protect rank-and-file officers from losing their jobs when they speak the truth.

In Georgia, when a police officer chooses honesty, they must be wary of corrupt colleagues. An honest officer must be financially prepared to endure as dishonest cops hold onto their jobs. Honesty in American policing is costly, especially for an officer with a family. Reputation is another concern. Depending on the rank of the corrupt officer, the destroyed reputation of the honest officer can overshadow the actual truth. Regaining that reputation, even after an investigation, is nearly impossible.

When a corrupt officer goes 'rogue' from the majority of clean officers, they are often referred to as 'dirty.' What happens when honest officers speak out about corruption in an agency? These officers, too, are considered 'rogue' for breaking the blue line of silence. The "thin blue line" is supposed to stand firm against criminality, not align with it.

Paul Harvey famously said, "...A policeman must know everything and not tell. He must know where all the sin is and not partake." Harvey's statement was only partially accurate. A police officer must speak up when necessary, especially when proper channels fail and the chain of command and state investigators refuse to take action. The public cannot have their trust shattered by the belief that officers are bribable. All officers are expected to remain above reproach in all aspects.

Georgia is facing a serious corruption problem. There are not enough incorruptible officers amidst the worst death rate in the War on Drugs. When police chiefs and other command staff can collaborate with state investigators to defame an honest officer, the public should be concerned. When that same officer, who did nothing wrong, is publicly labeled a liar, the public should be deeply worried. If an officer witnesses another confront a chief over illegal actions with zero consequences, the public should be afraid of what could happen to them.

If the system can do this to a police officer, despite clear evidence to the contrary, John and Jane Q. Public stand no chance. No amount of evidence, submitted to multiple authorities, stopped Georgia POST from posting a blatant lie, continuing to insist that whatever they say must be the truth because they cannot lie. Reflecting on Chatton and Ockham, as mentioned earlier in this book, nothing is black and white. Yet, Georgia POST would have the reader believe that their version of events is the only truth, and that Georgia POST itself is incapable of being manipulated by a Police Chief. Thus, they lied—

repeatedly—and continue to get away with it with complete impunity.

The only protection against overbearing management is labor representation. Georgia POST will not allow officers to form unions or collectively bargain, leaving POST staff and the Council with unfathomable power. They can not only create illegal policies but also violate laws openly and with impunity, knowing they will face no consequences. Police chiefs can flaunt their power, manipulating and controlling rank-and-file officers. This is not only illegal under state and federal laws, but goes directly against what policing should represent—not only to the public but to the profession meant to uphold the laws and protect societal ideals.

This leads to the ultimate question for Georgia's police officers: Who will stand up for the common citizen when the police cannot even stand for themselves?

The solution? Only the legislature can rein in such unchecked power. Only the General Assembly can protect Georgia from overbearing officers. While the best government may indeed be one closest to the people, with no oversight or checks on power, there's no telling what such governments are capable of. With unlimited power and the ability to lie without consequence, who would believe the common citizen? Especially when the words of three police officers, all telling the same story with proven evidence, are no match against the lies of a police chief.

The reader must decide for themselves the truth of the events that took place in Southwest Georgia from the spring of 2022 through to spring 2025—nearly three years of corruption, lies, and malfeasance. The author asks readers not to judge the profession as a whole. Most police officers remain honest and hardworking. Law enforcement is noble, and while the profession does make mistakes, the individuals highlighted in this account are the exceptions, not the rule.

The author also wishes to apologize to the public for the actions of a few officers. Larry Whisenant, Frank Walker, and Douglas Dowdy should never have become police officers, but who could have predicted they would engage in such behavior? Police officers are only as good as the information they receive, and these three individuals maintained a well-crafted façade for a long time. They even deceived other officers.

AFTERMATH

In December of 2022, following a lawsuit filed against the City of Poulan by John Masters for wrongful termination, Poulan Police Assistant Chief Frank Walker quietly retired from law enforcement altogether. As of the publication of this book, no investigation into Walker's actions has taken place.

In January of 2024, the City of Poulan sent a letter to Georgia POST, altering John Masters' separation from the City of Poulan from "Terminated" to "Voluntary Resignation" as part of a settlement to avoid both a court case and public exposure. In the settlement, Poulan admitted to "damages." Despite this official correspondence from the City of Poulan, the File Review remained in-place.

In October of 2024, Georgia POST violated POST policy and state law by releasing a copy of the investigative narrative and proposed POST discipline to a lawyer who had not represented Masters for nearly six months. Masters was not legally served with this notice, but he was notified when the attorney forwarded it to him via email.

In November of 2024, the first edition of this book was published as a direct public response to Douglas Dowdy's 10 pages of false statements and fictitious storytelling, which Dowdy had inserted into the POST investigative notes along with the proposed discipline.

In December of 2024, Georgia Peace Officer Standards and Training Director Mike Ayers unexpectedly retired without ceremony, quietly cleaning out his desk during the holiday season and making no public announcement of his sudden departure. Ayers' deputy director, Chris Harvey, was promoted to the new POST

Director position without any public notice or ceremony.

In early January of 2025, POST took "No Action" on Masters' POST record, effectively ending the investigation. This decision came after multiple news agencies and independent journalists repeatedly questioned the validity of the POST File Review of Masters and the actions of both Larry Whisenant and Douglas Dowdy. As of this publication, the 10 pages of POST discipline have not been uploaded to Masters' POST record.

In late January of 2025, Terry McCormick was promoted to Deputy Director of Georgia Peace Officer Standards and Training.

In early February of 2025, Sergeant Paul Agnew quietly retired from the Hartwell Police Department after 32 years. No public announcements were made, as is typical in the area. He is now employed by the Franklin Springs Police Department in Franklin County, GA, though not in a supervisory role.

Zackery Watson is "In Good Standing" with Georgia POST but no longer works in law enforcement.

As of the publication of this edition, John Masters remains "In Good Standing" with Georgia POST and continues to maintain his certification and training. He is now actively employed with a law enforcement agency in the state of Georgia—an agency that was not involved in any of the events described in this book. He regularly identifies and apprehends individuals in possession of drugs and firearms, as well as impaired drivers, using ethical and lawful interdiction methods.

Masters is currently writing another book, in which he will share his expert-level opinions on the current state of law enforcement in the United States and the cultural changes needed within policing to better serve the nation's citizens and residents.

In February of 2025, over a month after ending the File Review, Georgia POST legally served Masters with a notice of hearing letter via certified mail. After consulting with an attorney, John learned that he had no legal recourse to request a hearing. The letter, dated February 19, 2025, was sent nearly six weeks after the conclusion of the File Review on January 9, 2025.

A Georgia law enforcement agency to which Masters had applied sent a letter on the same date, rejecting his application for a Deputy Sheriff position, seemingly coordinating their letter with Georgia POST. This certified notice is the only legal notice received from Georgia POST in regards to a hearing.

As of this publication, no serious investigation into the events that transpired in the Spring of 2022 (and afterward) has ever been conducted. The witness to many of these events, a certified peace officer "In Good Standing" with Georgia POST, has never been contacted by Georgia POST, despite his neutral status as a third party.

Larry Whisenant remains the Chief of Police in the City of Poulan. In December of 2022, the City Council awarded him for his long years of service to the City of Poulan.

The United States remains the largest global importer of cocaine.

APPENDIX

GEORGIA PEACE OFFICER STANDARDS AND TRAINING COUNCIL

Mike Ayers
Executive Director

Notification of Proposed P.O.S.T. Discipline

Charles Cox JR, ATTORNEY

October 18, 2024

RE: Proposed Sanction of JOHN W MASTERS' P.O.S.T. Certification(s) Status

<u>This shall constitute Offical Notice in this matter.</u>

The Georgia P.O.S.T. Probable Cause Committee met on October 15, 2024 and proposed the following sanction(s) be placed on your certification(s).

A NO ACTION Agency action sufficient

This *proposed* sanction(s) is not a decision of the Council; it is a *proposed* action from the Probable Cause Committee for Council to vote upon from. Please note this process has changed. You have the two (2) following options:

<u>Option 1:</u> You may accept the proposed sanction and do nothing. After the passage of 30 days from the date of this notification letter, the proposed sanction will go to the Full Council for a vote without further information from you for Council to consider. Your only option for a hearing thereafter would be to appeal the Full Council Recommendation with a hearing at the Office of State Administrative Hearings (OSAH). You will be sent an official **<u>Notice of POST Discipline</u>** following Council's vote with further instructions on how to appeal (contest) that outcome.

*If your sanction was in the form of probation and you do not wish to appeal, probation will automatically begin thirty (30) days following the Notification of POST Discipline.

<u>Option 2:</u> You may request a Pre-Hearing Conference within 30 days of the mailing of this Notification of Proposed POST Discipline. The Pre-Hearing Conference is **VOLUNTARY.** It is a one hour in-person conference with a POST Hearings Officer for the purpose of discussing your case and/or presenting new information that you would like Council to consider prior to their final vote concerning your sanction. If you choose this option, a POST Hearings Officer will contact you to schedule your Pre-Hearing Conference.

Following the Pre-Hearing Conference, you will receive a Notification of POST Discipline (the Full Council's decision regarding the sanction of your certification). You will also receive instructions on how to appeal (contest) Council's decision.

To request a Pre-Hearing Conference prior to Full Council's final vote, **<u>you must check Option 2 below and complete steps 1-3 in the instructions that follow.</u>**

Regardless of which option you choose, your case will ultimately go before Full Council for a final vote. If you wish to appeal (contest) Full Council's decision, you must notify POST in writing in accordance with the instructions provided on the Notification of POST Discipline letter.

Page 1 of 2

For POST Council,

Mike Ayers, Executive Director

Cc: File

WRITTEN EXPRESSION OF CHOSEN OPTION

○ I choose Option 1 and accept the proposed sanction. I do not request a Pre-Hearing Conference. My signature and date are below. I may scan and email this page to **petitions@gapost.org** with a "read receipt" or (2) Send this page via certified mail (with tracking) to Georgia POST Council, PO Box 349, Clarkdale, Georgia 30111-0349.

○ I choose Option 2 and request to have a Pre-Hearing Conference for the purpose of discussing and presenting additional information for Full Council's consideration. I understand that I must do all of the following within thirty (30) days in order to have a Pre-Hearing Conference:

1. Write or type a response admitting or denying each and every allegation in the enclosed Case Summary. The response must be sworn or verified under oath (i.e. signed by you in front of a notary public). Provide the response to POST using one of two options: (1) Either scan and email the documents to **petitions@gapost.org** with a "read receipt" or (2) Send the original documents via certified mail (with tracking) to Georgia POST Council, PO Box 349, Clarkdale, Georgia 30111-0349.
2. Pay the required $100 Pre-Hearing Conference fee to POST. Payments may be made online at www.gapost.org using a credit card or with a certified check/money order made payable to "Georgia POST Council", P.O. Box 349, Clarkdale, Georgia 30111-0349. Cash or checks (unless certified) will NOT be accepted.
3. Check OPTION 2 under Written Expression of Chosen Option on page 2. Sign and date the bottom of the page. Send page 2 along with your written or typed response to POST using one of the methods described above.

If all 3 steps are not complete within the 30 days, the action will go before Full Council without any additional or mitigating information from you, and your right to be heard by Full Council will be waived. More detailed instructions may be found at http://www.gapost.org/appeal.html.

X ______________________________ X ______________ (date)

Signature of Officer

JOHN W MASTERS Officer Key [redacted]

Page 2 of 2

PROBABLE CAUSE COMMITTEE RECOMMENDATION TO COUNCIL
Investigations Division

Case No. 005-980-06-22

On 06/29/2022, POST received notification that Officer John W. Masters had been terminated by the Poulan Police Department on 06/28/2022. Documentation indicated that Officer Masters had been terminated for a "history of lying to the Chief or about the Chief."

POST received notification from a law firm representing the City of Poulan requesting that Officer Master's POST status be changed from termination to voluntary resignation.

On 04/08/2022, Officer Masters reported that he stopped a vehicle because the driver of the vehicle had "reacted" to the presence of law enforcement. He said the vehicle had changed from the fast lane to the slow lane for no apparent reason. He said the driver was holding an object in her hand and appeared to be eating out of it. She also looked away from the officers when she drove by. He stopped the vehicle and talked to the driver, . Officer Masters said he smelled the odor of marijuana. Officer Masters said he learned her driver's license were suspended. He arrested searched her, and placed her in the back seat of his patrol car. Officer Zackery Watson arrived on scene.

Officer Masters and had a discussion regarding her suspended license. She asked Officer Masters if she could call someone to pick her vehicle up. Officer Masters went to her car to get her telephone. While inside of the vehicle, he saw a bag containing a green, leafy substance and a pipe with burnt and green leafy substance on it. The officers searched the vehicle and found a yellow pill bottle with no label and a bag containing twenty-six (26) pills. Officer Masters said that these pills were identified as hydrocodone and acetaminophen. Officer Watson found a large bag in the trunk of the vehicle and a white powdery substance that appeared to be cocaine.

Officer Masters transported Ms. Hallmark to the jail. According to Officer Master's report, she was charged with:

Possession of Marijuana less than one ounce;
Possession of a synthetic narcotic;
Trafficking in cocaine;
Drugs to be kept in the original container; and
Driving while license suspended.

On 12/12/2022, POST Investigator Dowdy talked to Poulan Police Chief Larry Whisenant. Chief Whisenant said that he was out of town when was arrested. He said that Officer Masters had sent him a picture of a white powdery substance and a test kit. Chief Whisenant said that the picture showed that the test kit was purple, and a positive test would have turned the test kit blue. He said he told the officers not to send the

bd/04/24/2024

PROBABLE CAUSE COMMITTEE RECOMMENDATION TO COUNCIL
Investigations Division

005-980-06-22

substance to the crime lab until he was able to see it himself.

When Chief Whisenant returned to his office he tested the substance. He said that he could tell by looking at the substance that it was not cocaine. Chief Whisenant said he tested the substance using two different field tests and both were negative for cocaine. On 04/11/2022, Chief Whisenant contacted Worth County Deputy Adam Celinski and asked him to conduct a field test on the substance. Deputy Celinski concluded that the field test was negative for cocaine.

Chief Whisenant said that when he told Officer Masters and Officer Watson about the tests, Officer Masters asked "what did I do with the cocaine." Officer Watson made a comment that this "looks fishy" to him.

Chief Whisenant said he told both officers that they needed to find a new job. Chief Whisenant said that he called the District Attorney's Office and the Georgia Bureau of Investigation to inform them of this incident.

Chief Whisenant said he gave both officers time to find a new job or be fired. On 05/12/2022, Chief Whisenant notified Officer Masters that his employment would end on 05/27/2022. Officer Masters appealed his termination, but it was unanimously upheld by the City of Poulan's Mayor and Council on 06/28/2022.

POST records indicated that Officer Watson resigned from the Poulan Police Department on 05/02/2022. He was not subjected to a POST investigation.

On 06/28/2022, Chief Whisenant showed Deputy Celinski photographs of the test kit Officer Masters had sent Chief Whisenant. Deputy Celinski said that the test kit appeared to be negative for cocaine because it had turned purple instead of blue. Deputy Celinski submitted a statement regarding his opinion of the test kits.

According to the GBI Division of Forensic Sciences, the white powdery substance was not cocaine. The pills were positively identified as hydrocodone. There was no mention of the green leafy substance.

Court documents indicated that all charges against ██████ were dismissed by Assistant District Attorney Sandra Guest on 12/08/2022.

On 12/13/2022, this investigator talked to Officer Zachery Watson. Officer Watson said that he had backed Officer Masters up at a traffic stop where drugs were found in the car. He said the white powdery substance was field tested and the test result was positive for cocaine. He said that when he and Officer Masters met with Chief Whisenant, he told

bd/04/24/2024

Page 4 or 10

PROBABLE CAUSE COMMITTEE RECOMMENDATION TO COUNCIL
Investigations Division

005-980-06-22

them that he had retested the substance and the substance was not cocaine. Officer Watson said that he and Officer Masters questioned him about the cocaine, and Chief Whisenant asked them why they would not take his word for it. Officer Watson said that he told the Chief that he couldn't trust him.

On 12/14/2022, this investigator called Special Agent Kim Baker. She is the Special Agent in Charge of the Georgia Bureau of Investigations, Region 15. SAC Baker said that she was aware of the situation, and there was no investigation.

On 03/13/2024, POST Investigator Dowdy talked to Officer Masters. Officer Masters said that he had sued the city (Poulan) for wrongful termination. He said that the case was settled out of court and the city (Poulan) had agreed to change his POST status from terminated to voluntary resignation. He said that he was paid for the time he was on administrative leave. Officer Masters said that he was planning to leave the state and transfer his certifications. This investigator reminded him to keep his POST profile page updated. Officer Masters submitted a written response. (See attachment A).

On 04/02/2024, Investigator Dowdy called Shane Mims who is a drug investigator for the Tift County Sheriff's Office. Investigator Mims said that every cocaine field test kit he had ever used turned a bright blue if the substance being tested was positive for cocaine. He said that he had never seen a test that turned purple if the substance being tested was cocaine.

Chief Whisenant provided two examples of Officer Masters being untruthful:

On 04/03/2022, Chief Whisenant had a conversation with E-911 Director Doranda Chambless. Director Chambless said that Officer Masters had told her that Chief Whisenant had told the Poulan Police Officer to "call E911 if anything big was happening in Sylvester or the County," so that officers from the Poulan Police Department could respond also, if needed. Director Chambless said that Officer Masters had told her that Chief Whisenant had talked with the Sylvester Police Chief. She said Officer Masters had told her "My Chief met with SPD's Chief and anytime SPD is dispatched to a call that is a 10-10 or worse we are to key up and advise 911 we are available to respond, if we aren't doing anything." Chief Whisenant said that he had never said that to any of his officers.

On 04/04/2022, Officer Masters told Chief Whisenant that he was offered $3,000.00 to go to work for the Pelham Police Department. On 05/14/2022, Chief Whisenant talked to Pelham Police Captain Adam Lamb and he asked Captain Lamb about this. Captain Lamb told Chief Whisenant that the Pelham Police Department was not giving hiring bonuses at that time and he had never told Officer Masters that he would give him money

bd/04/24/2024

PROBABLE CAUSE COMMITTEE RECOMMENDATION TO COUNCIL
Investigations Division

005-980-06-22

to go to work for the Pelham Police Department.

The interviews conducted by Investigator Dowdy with Chief Whisenant and Officer Masters were digitally recorded. Two DVD's were placed in the POST file and they contain the documentation and recorded interviews.

Oglethorpe County Sheriff's Office

Officer Masters was employed by the Oglethorpe County Sheriff's Office from 07/11/2022 thru 08/19/2023.

On 08/16/2023, Officer Masters was involved in a single vehicle accident while operating his patrol vehicle. Officer Masters told his supervisor that something had ran out in front of him and he lost control of his vehicle. This information was passed on to the Madison County deputy who reported this in his accident report. Oglethorpe County Captain Ernest Ruark reviewed the in-car camera video and he did not see anything pass in front of Officer Master's police vehicle. Captain Ruark reported that he reviewed the driver's camera and he found that Officer Masters was using his cell phone and "changing the music" when the accident occurred.

On 08/17/2023, Captain Ruark talked to Officer Masters and asked him about the accident. Captain Ruark asked Officer Masters what happened, and at first, Officer Masters said that he did not know what happened. Then Officer Masters said that something came out in front of him and he lost control of his vehicle. Officer Masters did not say anything about being on his cell phone.

Captain Ruark also reported that on 07/29/2022, Officer Masters reported that a vehicle was fleeing from him. Captain Ruark reviewed the video and found that Officer Masters had activated his camera equipment after travelling a couple of miles prior to stopping the vehicle. Officer Masters claimed that he had turned on his blue lights while he was turning around. According to Captain Ruark, it appeared that the driver had pulled over immediately after Officer Masters activated his blue lights.

The Oglethorpe County Sheriff's Office wrote:

> Due to the incidents that have occurred, The Oglethorpe County Sheriff's Office sees that your services at this Office is no longer needed. We do understand about family and their needs. We do not want to have to terminate someone because of what it looks like on POST. Therefore the Sheriff's Office will be paying you for the next 30 days so you can find work somewhere else. We will expect a letter of resignation from you. If the letter is not submitted, then everything has to be sent

bd/04/24/2024

PROBABLE CAUSE COMMITTEE RECOMMENDATION TO COUNCIL
Investigations Division

005-980-06-22

to POST. We like to avoid this because we know how hard things can get. [sic]

POST Investigator Dowdy talked to Captain Ruark regarding these incidents. Captain Ruark said that his Sheriff had allowed Officer Masters to resign before any disciplinary action was taken against him. That was why the termination documents were not signed by Officer Masters.

Investigator Dowdy requested a copy of the videos regarding these incidents. On 04/17/2024, Office Manager Marteca Adkins advised that she was unable to locate the videos associated with these incidents.

POST records indicated that Officer Masters voluntarily resigned from the Oglethorpe County Sheriff's Office on 08/19/2023.

Hartwell Police Department

Officer Masters was employed by the Hartwell Police Department from 09/21/2023, until 01/03/2024. Chief Anthony Davis said that Officer Masters quit without giving proper notice. According to Chief Davis, Officer Masters was instructed to meet with him and Sergeant Paul Agnew at 10:00 AM on 01/03/2024, to discuss an email from Major Stan Sayer. This is a copy of the contents of the email:

From Sergeant Agnew to Major Sayer:
12/20/2023 11:30 AM

Let's begin with the video of Masters recording me with Joanie Haley. He pulled her over for speeding. He accidentally hit her car with his flashlight and called me to come assist. He notified me over the radio that he was going stat 8. Yet in his recording he repeated multiple times that I was letting her out of her ticket and she "found the right officer to get out of a ticket". He also insinuated that something inappropriate was occurring when she gave me a hug. This event leads me to believe that he is very much untrustworthy. I have known her all our lives and she was upset. She and I also attend the same church. If he had not already told me he was going stat 8 it would have likely ended differently as I told him if she was speeding, then she was speeding. He narrated the is event on his body camera . Right after he started on night shift he spent a few hours talking to some third shift deputies after doing so he met with myself, Trevor, Ed and Brittney at the Fairview building at shift change and announced to Ed that "he was not kidding about Hart county and the rumor mill" When I asked him about the rumors with the county he denied ever saying that. Recently he arrested an individual and dropped their belongings including a large amount of cash of

bd/04/24/2024

PROBABLE CAUSE COMMITTEE RECOMMENDATION TO COUNCIL
Investigations Division

005-980-06-22

roughly $1,000 in a paper bag in the hallway. When he was told that is not how things are done, he said that I never showed him what to do with arrestee's belongings. I have not only told him, but I have walked him through the procedure multiple times. He also has watched me do the procedure myself. But he is incapable of taking blame for any wrongdoing. He must have someone else to blame or he hits the roof.

He pulled over a car and found less than a half ounce of marijuana. He then saw a weapon and charged the individual with possession of a firearm during the commission of a crime. I told him this was the wrong charge. He continued with what he wanted to do. When 02 asked him about the charge, he told 02 that the boy told him he was going to go smoke the pot with his cousin. I have watched the video .... I did not hear that being said in the video. Masters says what he needs to say to accomplish what he wants to do. He informed myself, my wife, dispatch, and several other officers that 02 stated he was the "golden boy" of nightshift. When I referenced this to 02 via phone, he did not appear to know anything about saying any such thing.

The very next week, he began bragging that Gracie told him dayshift was bragging about him and saying he was known as "the hunter". When I mentioned this to Gracie, she knew nothing about saying any such thing to him. He was bragging about being a "bullet catcher" in the army. My wife stated she served in Naval Intelligence and maintained a top secret clearance. His very next statement was "well they pulled me off the front lines and gave me a clearance and lie detector test for the CIA." His story changes depending on who he is with and what other people have done.

You asked yesterday 12/19/23 about some of his specific lies and here are a few.

Paul Agnew

From Sergeant Agnew to Major Sayer:
12/20/2023 1:33 PM

Masters told me that he is the golden boy in front Desaray. Ginger Powell got onto him for dropping the money in the brown bag with inmate clothes. I don't remember the inmates name. He told Ginger that he was not properly trained on taking inventory of inmates property, and that is another lie because I trained him and showed him. On the hunter incident, he told me that Gracie said that dayshift was calling him the hunter. When I asked Gracie about it, she denied ever hearing anything like that.

bd/04/24/2024

PROBABLE CAUSE COMMITTEE RECOMMENDATION TO COUNCIL
Investigations Division

005-980-06-22

From Major Sayer to Sergeant Agnew:
005-980-06-22

12/20/2023 12:46 PM

Thanks! I will review the referenced cases that are recorded. In regards to the dropping belongings in booking, do you know the name or arrest date? Who was the dispatcher and officers during the" golden boy" claim? In regards to being referenced "the hunter", who were the officers?

He will be moved after the Christmas holidays.

From Major Sayer to Sergeant Agnew:
12/20/2023 3:21 PM

Got it, thanks.

Chief Davis to Officer Masters and other officers:
01/02/2024 4:27 PM

Meeting in my office at 10:00 with John Masters 1928 and Paul Agnew. About the email that Major Sayer sent. Thank you for the job that you do. Chief Davis

On 01/03/2024, Chief Davis received the following email from Officer Masters:

Effective 01/03/2024 I, John Masters, am no longer employed with the City of Hartwell Police Department. I turned in the keys to the vehicle and the door pass badges with dispatch and secured all issued equipment in the vehicle (including both firearms in the trunk), after parking it at City Hall last night.

Respectfully submitted,

John Masters

[sic]

POST documents indicated that Officer Masters voluntarily resigned on 01/03/2024.

bd/04/24/2024

Page 9 or 10

PROBABLE CAUSE COMMITTEE RECOMMENDATION TO COUNCIL
Investigations Division

005-980-06-22

DISCIPLINARY HISTORY

Date: 12/08/2023
Offense: Speeding and improperly executing a felony vehicle pullover.
Action taken: Recommended that Officer Masters receive remedial training regarding felony vehicle pullovers.

CRIMINAL HISTORY

None

VIOLATION

It is hereby asserted this individual is in violation of the following sections of O.C.G.A. 35-8-7.1 (a)(2),(6),(7),(11) as attached:

In accordance with O.C.G.A. 35-8-7.1 (b) (1), the Probable Cause Committee makes the following recommendation to the Council:

Chairman Probable Cause Committee
Date:

Chairman, POST Council
Date:

bd/04/24/2024

Page 10 or 10

ACKNOWLEDGMENT

My sincere thanks to the primary editors: Ryan Lassler, Paul Rogers, and Zackery Watson. Other editors also provided invaluable assistance, though they preferred to remain unnamed. Their help was invaluable and deserves recognition. They reviewed multiple edits, generously taking time from their busy schedules, and played a crucial role in bringing this book to fruition. They continued their efforts in editing the second, expanded edition, and I am deeply grateful for their hard work and perseverance.

My deepest thanks to my family for their unwavering support and patience throughout this process. Thank you for allowing me the time and space to concentrate and complete this work. You are the best family anyone could ask for, and I am truly blessed to have you.

Thanks to the other two officers involved in this project, and to their families as well, for their patience and support throughout the process, including late-night phone calls and the lengthy publishing journey.

ABOUT THE AUTHOR

John Masters is a certified peace officer in the state of Georgia. He has received training in interdiction, traffic enforcement, speed detection, advanced DUI detection, and narcotics enforcement.

He previously served in the US Army, where he received training in diesel operations, supply logistics, combat protocol, and grant writing. He deployed to Iraq and Afghanistan in support of the Global War on Terror. He is a lifetime member of the Veterans of Foreign Wars, in recognition of his service. He received an honorable discharge from the US Army along with the following awards: Army Commendation Medal, Army Good Conduct Medal, National Defense Service Medal, NATO Service Medal, Afghanistan Campaign Medal, Iraq Campaign Medal, Global War on Terrorism Service Medal, Army Service Ribbon, and Overseas Service Ribbon.

As a police officer, he performed high-risk warrant executions and traffic interdiction. Additionally, he worked in traffic and DUI enforcement, grant writing, and car seat education and safety. He also taught free classes to caregivers on car seat safety and maintained a grant program providing free car seats to caregivers in need.

He is actively employed in Law Enforcement in the state of Georgia. He is currently writing a book addressing modern-day issues preventing the effectiveness of law enforcement. It is schedule to be released in the fall of 2025.

Originally from the Midwest, he spent nearly all of his adult life in Alaska. He has also lived in Arizona, California, Utah, Missouri, and Oklahoma at various points in his life. He became a police officer in Georgia after his friend, John 'Uicimall'eq' Eubank, was murdered at Ft. Stewart, GA, in 2013.

Aside from Alaska, Georgia is the longest he has lived in one place, and it has become his second home.

www.ingramcontent.com/pod-product-compliance
Lightning Source LLC
LaVergne TN
LVHW022053200926
848481LV00003B/892

* 9 7 9 8 9 9 2 0 4 1 2 7 9 *